Mastering PHP Dependency Management with Composer

W G T AVINDA

DEDICATION

This book is dedicated to all the PHP developers and engineers who are striving to build high-quality, scalable, and maintainable PHP applications. Your commitment to mastering PHP dependency management is inspiring, and this book is a testament to your hard work and dedication.

I would also like to thank my family, friends, and colleagues for their unwavering support and encouragement throughout this project. Your love and support have been a constant source of inspiration and motivation, and I am truly grateful for all that you do.

Finally, I would like to thank the PHP community for their continued innovation, collaboration, and passion for open-source technology. Your contributions to the PHP ecosystem are invaluable, and I am honored to be a part of this vibrant and dynamic community.

Thank you all for your support, and I hope this book will serve as a valuable resource and guide on your journey towards mastering PHP dependency management.

W.G.T AVINDA

CONTENTS

ACKNOWLEDGMENTS

Writing a book is a team effort, and I am grateful to the many people who contributed to this project in countless ways.

First and foremost, I would like to thank my editor for their guidance, feedback, and support throughout the entire writing process. Your attention to detail, expertise, and enthusiasm have been invaluable, and I am honored to have had the opportunity to work with you.

I would also like to thank the technical reviewers who generously shared their insights, knowledge, and expertise on PHP dependency management. Your feedback, comments, and suggestions have helped make this book a more accurate, comprehensive, and useful resource for PHP developers.

Additionally, I would like to express my gratitude to the PHP community for their ongoing support and encouragement. Your passion, creativity, and generosity have inspired me to continue learning and growing as a developer, and I am honored to be a part of this vibrant and dynamic community.

Finally, I would like to thank my family, friends, and colleagues for their unwavering support and encouragement throughout this project. Your love, encouragement, and understanding have been a constant source of inspiration and motivation, and I am grateful for all that you do.

Thank you all for your support, and I hope this book will serve as a valuable resource and guide on your journey towards mastering PHP dependency management.

W.G.T AVINDA

1 INTRODUCTION TO PHP DEPENDENCY MANAGEMENT

In recent years, PHP has grown to become one of the most popular programming languages in the world. It's an open-source, server-side language that's used by millions of developers to build web applications, content management systems, and e-commerce sites. One of the reasons for PHP's popularity is its vast ecosystem of libraries, frameworks, and tools that help developers build more robust and scalable applications.

However, as projects become larger and more complex, managing dependencies can quickly become a daunting task. Dependency management is the process of identifying and managing external libraries and frameworks that your PHP application relies on. It involves installing, updating, and resolving conflicts between different versions of these dependencies.

In this book, we'll dive into the world of PHP dependency management and explore some of the best practices and tools for managing dependencies in your projects. We'll cover everything from the basics of dependency management to more advanced topics like versioning, resolving conflicts, and automating dependency management tasks.

Will serve as an introduction to PHP dependency management. We'll start by defining what dependency management is and why it's important for PHP developers. We'll also take a look at some of the common challenges that developers face when managing dependencies in their projects.

Section 1.1: What is Dependency Management?

Dependency management is the process of managing external libraries and frameworks that your PHP application relies on. When you're building a web application, it's likely that you'll use third-party libraries and frameworks to help you achieve your goals. These dependencies may be open-source or proprietary, and they may be hosted on various package managers, including Composer, PEAR, and PECL.

Managing these dependencies can be a difficult task, especially as your application grows in size and complexity. You need to ensure that all the dependencies are installed correctly and are up-to-date, and that there are no conflicts between different versions of the same library.

Section 1.2: Why is Dependency Management Important?

Dependency management is essential for several reasons:

1. **Code reusability:**
   Using external libraries and frameworks allows you to reuse code and avoid reinventing the wheel.
2. **Efficiency:**
   By using pre-built libraries and frameworks, you can save time and focus on building your application's core functionality.
3. **Security:**
   Using well-maintained and secure libraries can help you avoid common security vulnerabilities and reduce the risk of attacks.
4. **Scalability:**
   Managing dependencies effectively can help you build more scalable and maintainable applications.

Section 1.3: Common Challenges in Dependency Management

Despite the benefits of dependency management, it can be a challenging task for many developers. Some of the common challenges include:

1. **Versioning:**
   Managing dependencies across different versions can be tricky, especially when there are conflicts between different versions of the same library.
2. **Compatibility:**
   Ensuring that all your dependencies are compatible with each other and with your application can be a challenging task.
3. **Installation:**
   Installing and configuring dependencies can be a complex process, especially when dealing with multiple packages and libraries.
4. **Maintenance:**
   Keeping all your dependencies up-to-date and ensuring that your application is using the latest stable versions can be time-consuming.

In the following chapters, we'll explore some of the best practices and tools for managing these challenges and making PHP dependency management more manageable.

2 UNDERSTANDING PHP DEPENDENCIES

Before diving into the world of PHP dependency management, it's essential to have a clear understanding of what dependencies are and how they work. In this chapter, we'll explore the basics of PHP dependencies and how they're used in web development.

Section 2.1: What are Dependencies?

In PHP, a dependency is any external library, framework, or package that your application requires to function correctly. Dependencies can include PHP extensions, third-party libraries, and even other applications or services that your application interacts with.

When you're building a web application, it's essential to identify and manage all the dependencies that your application relies on. This can help you ensure that your application runs smoothly, and that any changes to dependencies won't cause issues in your codebase.

Section 2.2: Types of Dependencies

There are two main types of dependencies in PHP: **Direct** and **Indirect**.
Direct dependencies are packages or libraries that your application directly uses.

For example,
If you're building a Laravel application, Laravel itself is a direct dependency.
Other packages like PHPUnit or Carbon might also be direct dependencies.

Indirect dependencies, on the other hand, are packages or libraries that your direct dependencies rely on.

For example,
If you're using the Laravel framework, it relies on several other packages like Symfony components, which are indirect dependencies of your application.

It's essential to identify and manage both direct and indirect dependencies to ensure that your application functions correctly.

Section 2.3: Dependency Trees

When you have multiple dependencies in your application, it's essential to understand how they relate to each other. A dependency tree is a visual representation of all the dependencies in your application and their relationships.

In a dependency tree, the root node represents your application, and each subsequent node represents a dependency. Nodes are connected by edges that represent the dependency relationship between them.

Understanding your application's dependency tree can help you identify potential conflicts and ensure that all dependencies are installed and configured correctly.

Section 2.4: Package Managers

To manage dependencies in your PHP applications, you can use a package manager. A package manager is a tool that helps you install, update, and remove dependencies from your application.

Composer is the most popular package manager for PHP applications. It's a dependency manager for PHP that allows you to declare the dependencies of your project and automatically install them. Composer uses a central repository called Packagist, which hosts thousands of packages that you can use in your application.

Other package managers include PEAR and PECL, although they're not as widely used as Composer.

Section 2.5: Semantic Versioning

One of the most critical aspects of managing dependencies is understanding versioning. Semantic Versioning (SemVer) is a standardized way of versioning software that's widely used in the PHP ecosystem.

SemVer has three components: major version, minor version, and patch version. When a package's major version changes, it indicates a breaking change that's not backward compatible with previous versions. When the minor version changes, it indicates a new feature or enhancement that's backward compatible. Finally, when the patch version changes, it indicates bug fixes or other minor changes.

Understanding SemVer can help you identify potential conflicts between different versions of the same package and ensure that you're using the appropriate version of each dependency.

In the following chapters, we'll explore how to use package managers and other tools to manage PHP dependencies effectively. We'll cover everything from installing and updating dependencies to resolving conflicts and automating dependency management tasks.

Section 2.6: Dependency Injection

Dependency injection is a design pattern that's widely used in PHP web development to manage dependencies. It's a way of injecting dependencies into your application's classes rather than hard-coding them.

With dependency injection, your application's classes don't directly instantiate their dependencies. Instead, dependencies are injected into the class constructor or methods through parameters or setters.

Using dependency injection can help you decouple your application's classes from their dependencies, making them more modular and easier to test.

Section 2.7: Composer

Composer is the most widely used package manager for PHP applications. It's a dependency manager that allows you to declare the dependencies of your project and automatically install them.

With Composer, you declare your application's dependencies in a composer.json file. This file lists all the packages that your application needs, along with their required versions. Composer then reads this file and downloads and installs the required packages from the Packagist repository. Composer also allows you to specify constraints on the version of each package that you use.

For example, you can specify that you require version 2.0 of a package, and Composer will only install that version, even if a newer version is available.

Section 2.8: Composer Commands

Composer provides several commands that you can use to manage dependencies in your PHP applications. Here are some of the most commonly used Composer commands:

- **composer install:**
  Installs the dependencies listed in your composer.json file.
- **composer update:**
  Updates all the installed dependencies to their latest versions, based on the version constraints in your composer.json file.
- **composer require:**
  Adds a new dependency to your project.

- **composer remove:**
  Removes a dependency from your project.
- **composer outdated:**
  Lists all the dependencies in your project that have newer versions available.

Section 2.9: Composer Autoloading

Composer also provides a powerful autoloading mechanism that simplifies dependency management in your PHP applications. With autoloading, you don't need to manually include all the files for your application's dependencies. Instead, Composer takes care of loading the required files automatically.

To enable autoloading, you just need to include Composer's **autoload.php** file in your application's bootstrap process. Once autoloading is enabled, you can use any class from your application's dependencies without worrying about including the required files manually.

Section 2.10: Conclusion

In this chapter, we've explored the basics of PHP dependencies and how they're used in web development. We've looked at the different types of dependencies, dependency trees, and package managers like Composer. We've also covered Semantic Versioning, dependency injection, and Composer's autoloading mechanism.

Understanding PHP dependencies is essential for building robust and maintainable web applications. In the next chapter, we'll explore how to use Composer to manage dependencies effectively in your PHP projects

3 INTRODUCTION TO COMPOSER

In the previous chapter, we explored the fundamentals of PHP dependencies and their importance in web development. In this chapter, we'll dive deeper into Composer, the most popular dependency manager for PHP.

Section 3.1: What is Composer?

In the world of PHP, Composer has become a popular dependency management tool. It has drastically changed the way PHP developers handle dependencies in their projects. Composer provides a convenient way to manage PHP packages and their dependencies. In this chapter, we'll discuss what Composer is and how it works.

3.1.1 Definition of Composer

Composer is a popular dependency management tool for PHP applications. It allows developers to easily manage their project dependencies and ensure that their projects are using the correct versions of the required packages. Composer is built on top of the PHP package manager, PEAR, and uses a package manager called Packagist to manage packages.

With Composer, developers can specify the exact versions of packages that their projects require and easily install, update, or remove them. It also provides an autoloader that automatically loads the classes and files needed for a particular package, making it easier to manage and use the packages in your project.

Composer uses a configuration file called **composer.json** to specify the project's dependencies and their versions. The file also includes other project-specific information, such as the name and description of the project, the license, and any scripts that need to be run during installation or updates.

Overall, Composer simplifies the process of managing dependencies in PHP projects, making it easier for developers to build and maintain high-quality applications.

3.1.2 Purpose of Composer

Composer is a tool for managing dependencies in PHP applications. Its primary purpose is to simplify the process of managing and installing packages or libraries that your application relies on.

With Composer, you can easily declare the dependencies for your project in a configuration file (composer.json) and let Composer handle the installation and management of these dependencies for you. This makes it easier to manage complex projects with many dependencies, and also ensures that everyone on your team is working with the same set of dependencies.

Composer also helps to manage the version of packages that your application relies on, making it easy to upgrade or downgrade specific dependencies if needed. Additionally, Composer makes it easy to manage multiple versions of the same package, which is useful when working with legacy applications that require specific versions of dependencies.

Overall, Composer provides a convenient and efficient way to manage dependencies in PHP projects, helping to streamline development and ensure that your application is using the latest and most compatible versions of packages.

3.1.3 How Composer Works

Composer works by using a configuration file called composer.json, which defines the packages required by a project. The composer.json file contains information such as the package name, version, and dependencies. Composer uses this file to download and install the required packages and their dependencies. When a developer runs the Composer tool, it reads the composer.json file and fetches the required packages and their dependencies from the package repository. The packages are then installed into a folder called vendor, which contains all the required packages and their dependencies.

Composer also generates an autoloader file that automatically loads the required classes from the installed packages. This simplifies the process of including classes in the codebase, as the developer no longer has to manually include each file.

3.1.4 Benefits of Using Composer

Using Composer has many benefits for PHP developers. It simplifies the process of managing dependencies, reduces the likelihood of errors, and makes it easier to share code between projects. Some of the benefits of using Composer include:

- **Simplified package management:** Composer provides a unified and standardized way of managing PHP packages, making it easier to install, update, and remove packages in a consistent manner. This reduces the need for manual package management and helps ensure that packages are installed correctly with all required dependencies.
- **Dependency management:** Composer provides a powerful dependency management system that automatically installs the correct version of each package and its dependencies, based on the defined version constraints. This helps ensure that your application always uses the correct versions of its dependencies, which reduces the likelihood of conflicts and errors.
- **Automatic updates:** Composer can automatically check for updates to your packages and install the latest version when available, which helps keep your application up-to-date with security fixes and new features.
- **Faster development time:** By simplifying package management and dependency management, Composer can save developers time and effort, allowing them to focus on writing code instead of managing packages and dependencies.
- **Improved code quality and maintainability:** By using Composer to manage dependencies, developers can ensure that their code is built on a solid foundation of high-quality packages that are well-maintained and regularly updated. This can improve the overall quality and maintainability of the codebase.
- **Better collaboration and code sharing:** Composer makes it easy to share code between projects and with other developers. By using Composer to manage dependencies, developers can ensure that all required packages are installed and up-to-date, making it easier to collaborate on projects and share code with others.

Conclusion

Composer has become an essential tool for PHP developers. It simplifies the process of managing dependencies, improves code quality, and saves time. In the next chapter, we'll discuss the features of Composer in more detail.

Section 3.2: Features of Composer

Composer is a popular tool for managing PHP dependencies. It provides a number of features that make it an essential tool for modern PHP development.

1. **Dependency management:** Composer allows developers to specify the dependencies required by their project and automatically handles the installation and updating of those dependencies.
2. **Package management:** Composer provides access to a vast number of PHP packages available on Packagist, a repository of open-source packages for PHP. This makes it easy for developers to include third-party libraries and packages in their projects.
3. **Autoloading:** Composer provides a powerful autoloading feature that automatically loads PHP classes as they are needed. This means developers can easily use classes from the packages they include without needing to manually include them in their code.
4. **Version management:** Composer allows developers to specify version constraints for their dependencies. This ensures that the correct versions of packages are installed, preventing version conflicts and compatibility issues.
5. **Customization:** Composer provides a number of customization options, allowing developers to tailor its behavior to their specific needs. This includes options for specifying repositories, installing packages from local directories, and more.
6. **Scripting:** Composer includes a scripting feature that allows developers to define scripts that can be run during various stages of the dependency installation process. This can be used, for example, to run automated tests or perform other tasks.

Overall, Composer provides a powerful and flexible tool for managing dependencies in PHP projects. Its features make it easy for developers to include and manage third-party packages, ensuring that their projects remain up-to-date and maintainable.

Section 3.3: PEAR Dependency Management Tool

PEAR (PHP Extension and Application Repository) is a package manager for PHP applications. It was the first package manager for PHP and was introduced in 1999. PEAR provides a way to easily distribute and install PHP code and libraries.

The primary purpose of PEAR is to make it easier for developers to reuse code and avoid the need to write everything from scratch. PEAR packages provide a standardized way of organizing and sharing PHP code. Packages can be installed with the PEAR installer, which automatically handles dependencies and ensures that packages are installed correctly.

PEAR has many useful features, including:

1. **Packaging:** PEAR packages can be created using a simple command-line tool. Packages can include PHP code, documentation, and examples.
2. **Distribution:** PEAR packages can be distributed via a centralized repository, which makes it easy for developers to find and install packages.
3. **Dependency Management:** PEAR packages can specify dependencies on other PEAR packages, which simplifies the installation process.
4. **Upgrading:** PEAR packages can be easily upgraded to new versions.
5. **Compatibility:** PEAR packages are designed to work across a wide range of PHP versions and configurations.

PEAR has been widely used in the past, but its popularity has declined in recent years due to the emergence of other package managers like Composer. However, many legacy PHP applications still rely on PEAR packages, and it remains a valuable tool for managing PHP dependencies.

Section 3.4: PECL Dependency Management Tool

PECL (PHP Extension Community Library) is a repository that contains a collection of C extensions for PHP. These extensions are not written in PHP, but rather in C, which makes them run much faster and gives them access to low-level system resources.

PECL is not a dependency management tool, but rather a repository for PHP extensions. You can use PECL to install PHP extensions and add them to your PHP installation. This can be useful if you need to use a specific PHP extension that is not included in the default PHP installation.

To use PECL, you need to have the PECL command-line tool installed on your system. You can install it using the following command:

```
sudo apt-get install php-pear
```

Once you have PECL installed, you can use it to search for and install PHP extensions. For example, to install the memcached PHP extension, you can run the following command:

```
sudo pecl install memcached
```

After the installation is complete, you will need to add the extension to your PHP configuration file. You can do this by adding the following line to your php.ini file:

```
extension=memcached.so
```

Restart your web server to apply the changes.

PECL is not as widely used as Composer for dependency management in PHP projects, as it is more focused on installing and managing PHP extensions rather than PHP packages. However, it can be a useful tool for developers who need to use specific PHP extensions in their projects.

Section 3.5: Phing Dependency Management Tool

In addition to Composer, PEAR, and PECL, Phing is another popular dependency management tool for PHP. Phing is a build system written in PHP that allows developers to automate repetitive tasks in the software development process, such as building, testing, and deploying applications.

Phing is built on Apache Ant, a popular Java-based build tool, and it provides a set of tasks specific to PHP development. These tasks can be used to perform common tasks like running PHPUnit tests, creating documentation, and deploying an application to a remote server.

Phing also provides a way to manage project dependencies through the use of PEAR packages or Composer. Developers can specify the dependencies required for their project in a build file, and Phing will automatically download and install the necessary packages.

One of the main advantages of using Phing is that it provides a standardized way to automate the build process across different PHP projects. This can save developers a significant amount of time and effort, as they don't have to manually perform repetitive tasks for each project.

However, Phing is not as widely used as Composer, and it may not be the best choice for all projects. Developers should carefully evaluate their needs and requirements before deciding which dependency management tool to use.

You can download Phing from the official website at https://www.phing.info/. Once downloaded, you can install Phing by following the instructions provided on the website. Usually, you just need to extract the downloaded package to a directory of your choice, add the Phing bin directory to your system's PATH variable, and you're ready to use Phing for your project's build and deployment tasks.

Section 3.6: Installing Composer

Before you can use Composer, you'll need to install it on your system. Composer is a command-line tool, so you'll need to open a terminal or command prompt to install it.

First, you need to ensure that you have PHP installed on your system. You can check if PHP is installed by running the following command in your terminal or command prompt:

```
php -v
```

If PHP is installed, you should see its **version number** displayed. If not, you can download and install it from the official PHP website.

Once you have PHP installed, you can download the Composer installer using the following command in your terminal or command prompt:

```
php -r "copy('https://getcomposer.org/installer', 'composer-setup.php');"
```

This command will download the installer file into your current working directory.

Next, you need to run the installer using the following command:

```
php composer-setup.php
```

This will set up Composer on your system and create the composer.phar file in your current working directory.

Finally, you can move the composer.phar file to a directory in your system's PATH so that you can run Composer from any directory in your terminal or command prompt. For example, on a Unix-based system, you can move the file to **/usr/local/bin/composer** using the following command:

```
sudo mv composer.phar /usr/local/bin/composer
```

And that's it! You can now use Composer to manage dependencies in your PHP projects.

The installation process for Composer varies depending on your operating system. You can find detailed instructions on the Composer website.

Installation Linux Unix Macos

https://getcomposer.org/doc/00-intro.md#installation-linux-unix-macos

Composer can be installed on Windows, macOS, and Linux systems. To install Composer, follow these steps:

1. Download the Composer installer from the official website.

GetComposer.org, Download

https://getcomposer.org/download/

2. Follow the installation instructions for your operating system. For example, on Linux systems, you can install Composer using the following command:

    ```
    $ sudo apt-get install composer
    ```

3. Once Composer is installed, you can test it by running the following command:

    ```
    $ composer --version
    ```

    This should display the version of Composer that is installed on your system.

Section 3.7: Composer Basics

Composer is a dependency management tool for PHP that simplifies the process of managing and installing libraries and packages for your project. In this section, we will cover the basics of using Composer.

3.7.1. Creating a Composer Project

To create a new Composer project, you need to create a new directory and run the **composer init** command. This command will guide you through a series of prompts to configure your project and create a composer.json file, which is the main configuration file for Composer.

```
1    mkdir myproject
2    cd myproject
3    composer init
```

After running this command, you will be prompted to enter various details about your project, such as the name, description, author, license, and dependencies. You can also manually edit the composer.json file later to make changes.

3.7.2. Installing Dependencies

Once you have a composer.json file, you can install the dependencies for your project using the composer install command. This command will read the composer.json file and install all the required packages and their dependencies.

```
composer install
```

3.7.3. Updating Dependencies

If you need to update a package to a newer version or install a new package, you can modify the composer.json file and run the composer update command. This command will update all the packages listed in the composer.json file to their latest versions.

```
composer update
```

3.7.4. Autoloading

Composer provides an autoloading mechanism that automatically loads classes and functions as they are needed. This eliminates the need to manually include or require each file in your project.

To use autoloading, you need to add the following code to your PHP file:

```
1   <?php
2
3   require_once __DIR__ . '/vendor/autoload.php';
```

This code will load the Composer autoloader and make all the classes and functions available to your project.

3.7.5. Creating Scripts

Composer also allows you to define custom scripts that can be executed from the command line. These scripts can be used to perform various tasks, such as building the project, running tests, and deploying the project.

To define a script, you need to add the following code to your composer.json file:

```
2       "scripts": {
3           "build": "php build.php",
4           "test": "phpunit tests/"
5       }
```

In this example, we have defined two scripts: build and test. The build script will execute the **build.php** file, and the test script will run the PHPUnit tests located in the **tests/** directory.

To run a script, you can use the composer run command:

```
composer run build
```

This command will execute the build script defined in the composer.json file.

Here's another example composer.json file:

```
1    {
2        "require": {
3            "monolog/monolog": "^2.0",
4            "twig/twig": "^2.0"
5        }
6    }
```

In this example, we're declaring two dependencies: **monolog/monolog** and **twig/twig**. The ^2.0 notation means that Composer should install the latest version of each package that's compatible with version **2.0**.

To install the dependencies listed in your composer.json file, run the following command in your terminal or command prompt:

```
composer install
```

Composer will download and install all the required packages and their dependencies, creating a **vendor** directory in your project's root directory.

In this section, we covered the basics of using Composer. We learned how to create a new Composer project, install and update dependencies, use autoloading, and define custom scripts. Composer is a powerful tool that simplifies the process of managing dependencies in PHP projects, and it is widely used in the PHP community.

Section 3.8: Updating Dependencies

Once you've installed your application's dependencies, you can update them by modifying your **composer.json** file and running the following command:

```
composer update
```

This command updates all the installed dependencies to their latest versions based on the version constraints in your **composer.json** file.
You can also update a specific package by running the following command:

```
composer update <package-name>
```

Here are some of the most commonly used Composer commands:

- **composer install:** Installs the dependencies specified in the composer.json file.
- **composer update:** Updates the installed dependencies to their latest versions.
- **composer require:** Adds a new dependency to the composer.json file and installs it.
- **composer remove:** Removes a dependency from the composer.json file and uninstalls it.
- **composer show:** Lists the installed packages and their versions.
- **composer dump-autoload:** Regenerates the autoloader file, which is used to automatically load classes.

Section 3.9: Adding Dependencies

Adding dependencies is a crucial aspect of PHP dependency management. In this section, we will discuss how to add a new dependency to your project using Composer.

When you need to add a new dependency to your project, you must first identify the package name and version that you want to install. You can search for packages on the Packagist website, which is the main repository for Composer packages.

Once you have identified the package you want to install, you can add it to your project using the composer require command. For example, let's say you want to add the **guzzlehttp/guzzle package** to your project. You can run the following command:

```
composer require guzzlehttp/guzzle
```

This command will automatically update your composer.json file and install the **guzzlehttp/guzzle** package and its dependencies. The composer.json file will now include a new entry in the require section, which looks something like this:

```
1  {
2      "require": {
3          "php": "^7.1.3",
4          "guzzlehttp/guzzle": "^7.0"
5      }
6  }
```

The version constraint specified for the **guzzlehttp/guzzle** package (**^7.0**) means that Composer will install any version of the package that is compatible with version **7.0**, but not version **8.0** or later.

You can also specify the version of the package that you want to install using a more specific version constraint. For example, if you want to install version **7.3.0** of the **guzzlehttp/guzzle** package, you can run the following command:

```
composer require guzzlehttp/guzzle:7.3.0
```

This will update your composer.json file and install version **7.3.0** of the **guzzlehttp/guzzle** package.

Once the new package and its dependencies are installed, you can use them in your PHP code by including the relevant classes and functions from the package.

In summary, adding a new dependency to your project involves identifying the package name and version, and then using the composer require command to update your composer.json file and install the new package and its dependencies.

Section 3.10: Removing Dependencies

Removing dependencies is an important part of managing your project's dependencies, as you may no longer need a particular package, or you may need to replace it with a different package that provides similar functionality.

To remove a dependency from your project, you can use the composer remove command, followed by the name of the package you want to remove.

For example,
To remove the **monolog/monolog** package from your project, you can run the following command:

```
composer remove monolog/monolog
```

This will remove the monolog/monolog package from your project's dependencies and update the composer.json file to reflect this change. Composer will also remove the package from the vendor directory.

It's important to note that when you remove a package, you may also need to update your code to remove any references to that package.

For example,
If you had been using the **monolog/monolog** package in your code, you would need to update your code to remove any references to it, or replace them with references to a different package that provides similar functionality.

Another consideration when removing dependencies is to ensure that you don't accidentally remove a package that is still needed by other packages in your project. Composer will notify you if a package you want to remove is still required by another package and will not allow you to remove it until you resolve the issue.

In addition to removing individual packages, you can also remove entire groups of packages by updating the composer.json file directly. For example, you can remove all development dependencies from your project by removing the require-dev section from the composer.json file.

Section 3.11: Autoloading

Composer provides an autoloading mechanism that simplifies the process of including files for your application's dependencies. With autoloading, you don't need to manually include all the files for each package in your project.

To use autoloading, add the following line to your project's bootstrap file (usually index.php):

```
1   <?php
2
3   require_once __DIR__ . '/vendor/autoload.php';
4
```

This line loads the Composer autoloader, which automatically includes the files for all the packages in your project.

Here is an example of how to use Composer to install the dependencies required by a PHP project:

1. Create a new composer.json file in the root directory of your project, and add the required dependencies to it.
   For example:

```
1   {
2       "require": {
3           "monolog/monolog": "^2.0",
4           "twig/twig": "^3.0"
5       }
6   }
```

2. Run the composer install command in the terminal. This will download and install the required packages, and generate the autoloader file.
3. Use the installed packages in your PHP code.

For example,
To use the Monolog package, you can add the following code to your PHP file:

```
1   <?php
2
3   require_once __DIR__ . '/vendor/autoload.php';
4
5   use Monolog\Logger;
6   use Monolog\Handler\StreamHandler;
7
8   $log = new Logger('name');
9   $log->pushHandler(new StreamHandler('path/to/your.log', Logger::WARNING));
10  $log->warning('Foo');
11  $log->error('Bar');
```

This code creates a new logger object using the Monolog package, and logs warning and error messages to a file.

Section 3.12: Composer Scripts

Composer also allows you to define custom scripts that run before or after certain Composer commands. These scripts can be used to perform tasks such as compiling assets, running tests, or generating documentation.

To define a script, add a scripts section to your composer.json file, like this:

```
1   {
2       "scripts": {
3           "post-install-cmd": [
4               "php bin/console doctrine:migrations:migrate",
5               "npm install",
6               "npm run build"
7           ],
8           "post-update-cmd": [
9               "php bin/console doctrine:migrations:migrate",
10              "npm install",
11              "npm run build"
12          ]
13      }
14  }
```

In this example,
We're defining two scripts that run after the install and update commands, respectively. These scripts run the Doctrine migrations, install and build the JavaScript assets using npm.

Section 3.13: Composer Best Practices

When working with Composer, it's important to follow best practices to ensure the stability and security of your application. Here are some best practices to keep in mind:

1. **Always use the latest version of Composer:** Composer is constantly being updated with new features and bug fixes, so it's important to make sure you are using the latest version.
2. **Declare all dependencies in your composer.json file:** This ensures that your project's dependencies are clearly documented and that other developers working on the project can easily see what dependencies are required.
3. **Use version constraints:** Version constraints allow you to specify the version range of a dependency that your project can use. This ensures that your project stays compatible with the required version of the dependency.
4. **Use composer.lock file:** The composer.lock file contains a record of the exact versions of all the packages installed in your project. This file should be committed to version control so that all developers on the project are working with the same set of dependencies.
5. **Regularly update dependencies:** Regularly updating your project's dependencies ensures that you are always using the latest bug fixes and security patches.
6. **Use a private repository for proprietary code:** If you have proprietary code that you want to keep private, you can use a private repository to manage these dependencies.
7. **Test your application after updating dependencies:** Updating dependencies can introduce new bugs or conflicts, so it's important to test your application thoroughly after updating to ensure that everything is still working as expected.
8. **Use a dependency analyzer:** A dependency analyzer can help you identify potential conflicts or security vulnerabilities in your project's dependencies.

By following these best practices, you can ensure that your project's dependencies are managed efficiently and securely.

Section 3.14: Managing Versions with Composer

Managing versions of dependencies is an important aspect of dependency management in any software project. With Composer, you can manage the versions of your project's dependencies easily and efficiently. In this section, we'll explore how to manage versions with Composer.

Semantic Versioning

Before we dive into managing versions with Composer, it's important to understand semantic versioning (also known as SemVer). Semantic versioning is a widely used versioning system that ensures compatibility and consistency across different versions of software packages.

Semantic versioning consists of three numbers separated by periods: MAJOR.MINOR.PATCH. These numbers are used to represent different types of changes:

- **MAJOR** version changes indicate that the package has undergone significant changes that are not backwards-compatible with previous versions.
- **MINOR** version changes indicate the addition of new features or functionality that are backwards-compatible with previous versions.
- **PATCH** version changes indicate bug fixes or minor improvements that are backwards-compatible with previous versions.

It's important to follow semantic versioning when creating and updating software packages to ensure that users can easily upgrade to new versions without breaking their existing code.

Specifying Package Versions

With Composer, you can specify the versions of your project's dependencies using the version constraint syntax. This syntax allows you to specify a range of acceptable versions for a package.

The most common version constraint syntax is the tilde (~) and caret (^) operators. The tilde operator allows you to specify a minimum version and a maximum backwards-compatible version. For example, ~1.2.3 specifies any version greater than or equal to 1.2.3 but less than 2.0.0. The caret operator works similarly but allows for breaking changes in the MINOR version. For example, ^1.2.3 specifies any version greater than or equal to 1.2.3 but less than 2.0.0.

You can also specify exact version numbers or use comparison operators like >, >=, <, and <= to specify a range of acceptable versions.

Updating Package Versions

To update your project's dependencies to the latest versions, you can use the composer update command. This command will update all packages to their latest versions, based on the version constraints specified in your composer.json file.

If you want to update a specific package to a newer version, you can use the composer update command followed by the package name. For example, composer update monolog/monolog will update the monolog/monolog package to its latest version.

Lock File

Composer creates a lock file (composer.lock) to ensure that all dependencies are installed with the correct versions. This file contains the exact versions of all packages installed in your project, including their dependencies.

When you run the composer install command, Composer reads the lock file and installs the exact versions of all packages listed in the file. This ensures that all developers working on the project are using the same package versions.

Here are some examples of version constraints:

- **^2.0:**
  Allows any version greater than or equal to 2.0, but less than 3.0.
- **~2.0:**
  Allows any version greater than or equal to 2.0, but less than 2.1.
- **2.0.3:**
  Allows version 2.0.3 only.
- **>=2.0,<3.0:**
  Allows any version greater than or equal to 2.0, but less than 3.0.

By default, Composer installs the latest version of each package that is compatible with your project's version constraints. However, you can also specify a specific version of a package by using the @ symbol followed by the version number.

For example:

```
1    {
2        "require": {
3            "monolog/monolog": "1.25.0"
4        }
5    }
```

This composer.json file specifies that we want to use version 1.25.0 of the Monolog package.

```
2        "require": {
3            "monolog/monolog": "1.0.*@beta",
4            "acme/foo": "@dev"
5        }
```

Managing versions of your project's dependencies is crucial to ensure that your project is using compatible and consistent packages. With Composer, you can easily specify and manage the versions of your project's dependencies, ensuring that your project is using the correct package versions.

Conclusion

In conclusion, Composer is a powerful and widely used dependency management tool for PHP projects. It provides many features such as dependency resolution, autoloading, and version management, making it easy to manage the dependencies of your PHP projects.

Using Composer, you can easily add, remove, and update dependencies, and also manage versions and conflicts between dependencies. Additionally, Composer supports both public and private repositories, allowing you to manage both open-source and proprietary dependencies.

4 MANAGING DEPENDENCIES WITH COMPOSER

In the previous chapter, we introduced Composer and explored its basic features. In this chapter, we'll delve deeper into Composer and look at how to manage dependencies with it.

Section 4.1: Updating Dependencies

As we discussed in the previous chapter, Composer creates a composer.lock file that lists all the installed dependencies and their versions. When you run composer install, Composer installs the exact versions of each package specified in the **composer.lock** file.

However, what happens when you want to update a package to a newer version? In this case, you can run the composer update command. This command updates all packages to their latest versions that satisfy the version constraints specified in the **composer.json** file. After updating the packages, Composer generates a new **composer.lock** file that lists the updated versions.

It's important to note that updating packages can introduce incompatibilities or break your application if the updated package contains breaking changes. To avoid this, it's recommended to update packages in a development environment and thoroughly test the updated code before deploying to production.

Section 4.2: Installing Packages

Composer provides a simple and efficient way to install packages and manage dependencies in your PHP project. In this section, we will discuss how to install packages using Composer.

To install a package using Composer, you need to use the require command.

For example,

If you want to install the **monolog/monolog** package, you can run the following command in your terminal or command prompt:

```
composer require monolog/monolog
```

This will download the latest version of the monolog/monolog package and add it to your project's composer.json file. Composer will also create a vendor directory in your project's root directory, which contains all the dependencies required by your project.

You can also specify a specific version of a package to install using the following command:

```
composer require monolog/monolog:1.0.0
```

This will install version **1.0.0** of the **monolog/monolog** package.

You can also install multiple packages at once by specifying their names separated by spaces:

```
composer require monolog/monolog symfony/console guzzlehttp/guzzle
```

This will install the **monolog/monolog, symfony/console**, and **guzzlehttp/guzzle packages**.

Additionally, you can also install packages as dev dependencies by using the --dev flag:

```
composer require --dev phpunit/phpunit
```

This will install the **phpunit/phpunit** package as a development dependency, which means it will not be included in the production build of your project.

In summary, installing packages using Composer is a straightforward process that can be done with a single command. Composer takes care of resolving package dependencies and downloading the required packages from the internet, making it an essential tool for managing PHP dependencies in modern projects.

Section 4.3: Removing Packages

Removing packages is a common task when working with Composer. It can be necessary when a package is no longer needed, or when upgrading to a new version of a package that requires a different set of dependencies.

To remove a package, you can use the composer remove command followed by the name of the package you want to remove.

For example,

To remove the **monolog/monolog** package from your project, you can run the following command:

```
composer remove monolog/monolog
```

This command will remove the package from your project's composer.json file and uninstall it from your project's vendor directory.

If you want to remove a package and its dependencies that are no longer required by any other packages in your project, you can use the --no-require option.

For example:

```
composer remove monolog/monolog --no-require
```

This command will remove the package and all its dependencies that are no longer required by any other packages in your project. Note that this can also remove other packages that are not directly related to the package you are removing, so use this option with caution.

It's important to note that removing a package can break your project if other packages in your project depend on it. Before removing a package, it's a good idea to check if any other packages in your project depend on it and whether removing it will cause any issues. You can use the composer depends command to check the dependencies of a package.

```
composer depends monolog/monolog
```

This command will show you a list of packages that depend on the **monolog/monolog** package. If any of these packages are still required in your project, you may want to consider keeping the **monolog/monolog** package or finding an alternative package that meets your needs.

In summary, removing packages with Composer is a straightforward process that can be done with the composer remove command. However, it's important to be cautious when removing packages as it can potentially break your project if other packages depend on it.

Section 4.4: Installing Specific Versions

One of the key features of Composer is the ability to install specific versions of packages. This can be helpful if you need to maintain compatibility with a specific version of a package, or if you need to test your code against multiple versions of a package.

To install a specific version of a package, you can specify the version number when running the composer require command.

For example, to install version **2.0.0** of the **monolog/monolog** package, you would run the following command:

```
composer require monolog/monolog:2.0.0
```

You can also use a range of version constraints to specify which versions of a package to install.

The most common version constraints are:

1   ^: Allows the most recent minor version (i.e., the version number to the right of the first decimal point) but keeps the major version (i.e., the number to the left of the first decimal point) constant.
For example, ^2.0.0 would allow any version from 2.0.0 to 2.999.999 but not 3.0.0 or higher.

2   ~: Allows the most recent patch version (i.e., the version number to the right of the second decimal point) but keeps the major and minor versions constant.
For example, ~2.0.0 would allow any version from 2.0.0 to 2.0.999 but not 2.1.0 or higher.

3   **>=, >, <=, <:** Allows any version that meets the specified comparison operator.
For example, >=2.0.0 would allow any version 2.0.0 or higher.

4   *: Allows any version of the package.

For example, to allow any version of the **monolog/monolog** package that is compatible with version **2.0.0**, you would run the following command:

```
composer require monolog/monolog:^2.0.0
```

When you install a specific version of a package, Composer will generate a lock file (composer.lock) that specifies the exact version of each dependency that should be installed. You can commit this lock file to your version control system to ensure that all developers and servers are using the same versions of packages.

To install the packages specified in the lock file, you can run the composer install command. This will ensure that you have the exact versions of each dependency that you need.

Alternatively, you can install a package by specifying a Git branch, tag, or commit hash. For example, to install a package from a Git repository at a specific commit hash, you can run the following command:

```
composer require vendor/package:dev-master#abcdef
```

This command installs the **vendor/package** package from the **dev-master** branch at the **abcdef** commit hash.

Section 4.5: Using Private Packages

While Composer is widely used for managing dependencies for open-source projects, it is also a powerful tool for managing dependencies for private projects. In this section, we will explore how to use private packages with Composer.

Private packages are packages that are not publicly available on Packagist or any other public repository. These packages can be hosted on private repositories such as **GitHub, GitLab**, or **Bitbucket**.

To use private packages with Composer, you need to specify the repository where the package is hosted.

This can be done by adding a new entry to the repositories section in your composer.json file.

```
1   {
2       "repositories": [
3           {
4               "type": "vcs",
5               "url": "https://github.com/username/repo"
6           }
7       ],
8       "require": {
9           "username/repo": "dev-master"
10      }
11  }
12
```

In the above example,

We have added a new repository entry for a package hosted on **GitHub**. We have specified the repository type as **"vcs"** and provided the URL to the repository. We have also added the package to the require section using the **username/repo** format and specified the version constraint as **"dev-master"**.

Once you have added the repository entry and specified the package in the require section, you can install the package using the composer install or composer update command.

```
composer install
```

If the package requires authentication, you will need to provide your credentials to Composer. This can be done by creating a personal access token on the hosting platform and adding it to the composer.json file.

```
1   {
2       "config": {
3           "github-oauth": {
4               "github.com": "TOKEN"
5           }
6       }
7   }
```

In the above example,

We have added a new config section to the composer.json file and specified the **GitHub** OAuth token for authentication.

Using private packages with Composer can greatly simplify the process of managing dependencies for private projects. By hosting your own packages, you have full control over the versioning, updates, and security of your dependencies.

Private repository

In addition to installing packages from public repositories like Packagist, you can also install packages from private repositories. This is useful for companies or organizations that want to share code between their own projects but don't want to make the code publicly available.

Composer supports various private package repositories, including Satis and Toran Proxy. These tools allow you to create a private repository that hosts your own packages, which can be installed using Composer.

To use a private package repository with Composer, you need to specify the repository URL in your **composer.json** file.

For example,

If you're using Satis, you can add the following code to your **composer.json** file:

```
1  {
2      "repositories": [
3          {
4              "type": "composer",
5              "url": "https://example.com/satis/"
6          }
7      ]
8  }
9
```

This code specifies a private repository hosted at
https://example.com/satis/.
Once you've added this code to your composer.json file, you can install packages from the private repository using the composer require command, just like you would with public packages.

My-Project, composer.json

https://github.com/thusithawijethunga/php-dependency-manage-
ment/blob/main/satis-repository/my-project/composer.json

Section 4.6: Using Composer Autoloading

One of the key features of Composer is its ability to generate autoloading files for your project's classes, allowing you to easily use and reference them without having to manually include or require them in your code. This saves time and effort, and also helps to ensure that your code is well-organized and maintainable.

To use Composer autoloading, you first need to define the namespaces and directories for your project's classes in the composer.json file, using the **"autoload"** section.

For example:

```
1   {
2       "autoload": {
3           "psr-4": {
4               "MyNamespace\\": "src/"
5           }
6       }
7   }
```

This configuration tells Composer to look for classes in the **"src/"** directory and load them under the **"MyNamespace"** namespace. Note that the **"psr-4"** autoloading standard is used here, which maps the namespace to the directory structure in a predictable and consistent way.

Once you have defined your autoloading rules, you can generate the autoload files by running the following command in the terminal:

```
composer dump-autoload
```

This will generate a new file called **"vendor/autoload.php"** that contains all the necessary code to autoload your project's classes. You can then include this file at the beginning of your PHP scripts to make sure all the necessary classes are loaded:

```
1   <?php
2
3   require_once __DIR__ . '/vendor/autoload.php';
4
```

This line should be added at the beginning of any PHP file that uses classes defined in your project.

Composer also provides an alternative autoloading method called **"classmap"**, which allows you to specify individual files or directories to load all the classes in. This can be useful in cases where the class files do not follow the standard naming conventions, or when the classes are located in multiple directories. Here is an example configuration for classmap autoloading:

```
1  {
2      "autoload": {
3          "classmap": [
4              "src/MyClass.php",
5              "lib/OtherClass.php"
6          ]
7      }
8  }
```

This configuration tells Composer to load the **"MyClass.php"** file from the **"src/"** directory and the **"OtherClass.php"** file from the **"lib/"** directory.

In general, using the **PSR-4** autoloading standard is recommended, as it provides a more predictable and maintainable way to autoload classes. However, there may be cases where the classmap autoloading method is more appropriate, depending on your project's requirements.

Overall, Composer autoloading is a powerful feature that can greatly simplify your project's code structure and organization. By taking the time to set up and configure autoloading, you can save time and effort in the long run, and make your code more modular and maintainable.

Section 4.7: Managing Composer Cache

Composer uses a cache to store downloaded packages and their dependencies to speed up future installations and updates. The cache can be managed with the **composer clear-cache** command, which clears the cache and frees up disk space.

```
composer clear-cache
```

In addition, Composer also provides the ability to store packages globally on the system to reduce the amount of duplication across projects. This can be achieved by running the following command:

```
composer global require package/name
```

To remove a globally installed package, this can be achieved by running the following command:

```
composer global remove phpunit/phpunit
```

By default, Composer stores its cache in the **~/.composer/cache** directory on Unix-based systems or **%APPDATA%/Composer/cache** on Windows.

You can manage the cache in several ways:

1. Clear the entire cache using the **composer clear-cache** command. This will remove all cached packages and metadata.
2. Remove specific packages from the cache using the **composer clear-cache <package>** command. This will remove the cached package and its metadata.
3. Disable the cache for specific commands using the **--no-cache** option. For example, to disable the cache for the **install** command, run **composer install --no-cache**.
4. Change the cache directory using the **--cache-dir** option. For example, to set the cache directory to **/tmp/composer-cache**, run **composer install --cache-dir=/tmp/composer-cache**.
5. Use a custom cache directory for a specific package by setting the **cache-files-dir** option in the **composer.json** file. This option can be used to cache specific files that are frequently requested by the package.

It's important to note that the Composer cache is designed to be safe to delete at any time, and clearing the cache will not affect the functionality of your project or its dependencies. However, clearing the cache may slow down subsequent dependency resolution and installation operations as the cache needs to be rebuilt.

Section 4.8: Handling Conflicts with Composer

When using Composer to manage dependencies in your PHP project, you may encounter conflicts between different packages. Conflicts occur when two or more packages require different versions of the same package, or when two or more packages provide conflicting functionality.

Composer includes a built-in conflict resolution system to help you manage these conflicts. When a conflict is detected, Composer will attempt to resolve it by selecting the best possible version of each package that meets all of the requirements.

Here are some tips for handling conflicts with Composer:

1. Keep your dependencies up-to-date: It's important to keep your dependencies up-to-date to avoid conflicts caused by using outdated packages. Composer makes it easy to update your dependencies by running the **composer update** command.
2. Understand version constraints: Make sure you understand how version constraints work in Composer. By default, Composer uses semantic versioning (semver) to manage dependencies. This means that packages are versioned using a three-part scheme: major version, minor version, and patch version. You can specify version constraints in your **composer.json** file using a range of operators, including ~, ^, and >=.
3. Use the **composer why-not** command: If you encounter a conflict with Composer, you can use the **composer why-not** command to see why a certain package is being installed and what conflicts are preventing it from being installed.
4. Manually resolve conflicts: In some cases, you may need to manually resolve conflicts by editing your **composer.json** file. You can specify specific package versions or version ranges to resolve conflicts. Be careful when doing this, as it can lead to more conflicts down the line.
5. Use the **composer prohibits** command: The **composer prohibits** command can be used to list all packages that cannot be installed due to conflicts with existing packages.

6. **Use aliases:** If you have a package that requires a specific version of a dependency, but another package requires a different version, you can use aliases to create a separate version of the dependency for the conflicting package.

7. **Use the --no-update flag:** When installing or updating packages, use the --no-update flag to prevent Composer from automatically updating dependencies. This can help you avoid conflicts by allowing you to manually update dependencies one at a time.

8. **Use the --ignore-platform-reqs flag:** If you're running into conflicts due to platform requirements (e.g., a package that requires a specific version of PHP), you can use the --ignore-platform-reqs flag to bypass these requirements and install the package anyway. However, be aware that this can cause compatibility issues.

By following these tips, you can effectively manage conflicts when using Composer to manage dependencies in your PHP projects.

Use Aliases:

When working with large codebases or importing multiple namespaced classes, you may find that typing out the full namespace every time you reference a class can be time-consuming and error-prone. In PHP, you can use the "use" keyword to define an alias for a fully-qualified class name.

For example, instead of typing:

```
1   <?php
2
3   $logger = new Psr\Log\Logger();
4
```

You can define an alias for the **Psr\Log\Logger** class:

```
1   <?php
2
3   use Psr\Log\Logger;
4
5   $logger = new Logger();
6
```

You can also alias specific class methods, constants, and even function names:

```php
1    <?php
2
3    use Symfony\Component\Console\Output\ConsoleOutputInterface as OutputInterface;
4
5    $output = new OutputInterface();
6
```

In this example, we are importing the **"ConsoleOutputInterface"** class from the **"Symfony\Component\Console\Output"** namespace, but using an alias of **"OutputInterface"** for brevity.

Use aliases can make your code more readable and save you time and effort when typing out class names. However, it's important to use them judiciously and avoid creating overly generic aliases that could cause confusion or conflicts with other code.

Section 4.9: Creating Your Own Packages

Creating your own packages can be a powerful way to reuse code across projects and to share your work with others. Composer provides a straightforward way to create and publish your own PHP packages.

To create your own package, you first need to define its structure. Composer follows a convention-based approach for defining package structures, which is based on the PSR-4 autoloading standard.

Here are the steps to create a simple package using Composer:

1. Create a new directory for your package, and navigate to it in the command line.
2. Create a new composer.json file in this directory, and define the package name, version, and any dependencies. You should also define the autoloading rules for your package, using the PSR-4 standard.

   Here is an example of a composer.json file:

```
1   {
2       "name": "your-username/your-package-name",
3       "version": "1.0.0",
4       "description": "A short description of your package",
5       "authors": [
6           {
7               "name": "Your Name",
8               "email": "your.email@example.com"
9           }
10      ],
11      "require": {},
12      "autoload": {
13          "psr-4": {
14              "YourNamespace\\": "src/"
15          }
16      }
    }
```

3. Create a src directory, and place your PHP files inside it. These files should be namespaced according to the PSR-4 autoloading standard.

    For example, if you defined the autoloading rule

    "YourNamespace\\": "src/", then you should place your PHP files inside the **src/** directory, and namespace them as **namespace YourNamespace;**.

4. Commit your package to a version control system such as Git, and push it to a hosting service such as GitHub or GitLab.
5. Publish your package to Packagist, which is the main repository for Composer packages. To do this, you need to create an account on Packagist, and then add your package's repository URL to your account. Once your package is published to Packagist, it can be installed by other users using Composer.

Note that creating your own package can be a complex process, and there are many additional considerations to keep in mind. For example, you may want to include tests, documentation, and examples with your package. However, the basic steps outlined above should be enough to get you started.

Section 4.10: Understanding Composer's Dependency Resolution

Dependency resolution is one of the most important features of Composer. It is the process of determining which versions of dependencies should be installed based on the requirements specified in the composer.json file.

When you run the **composer install** or **composer update** command, Composer analyzes the dependencies specified in the **composer.json** file and the constraints specified in the **composer.lock** file (if it exists) to determine the exact versions of the required packages that need to be installed.

The process of dependency resolution involves several steps:

1. Reading the **composer.json** file to determine the required dependencies for the project.
2. Checking the **composer.lock** file (if it exists) to determine if any specific version constraints have already been specified.
3. Determining the latest version of the required package that matches the version constraints.
4. Resolving conflicts between different packages that have different version requirements or dependencies.
5. Creating a dependency tree that shows the relationships between all the required packages and their dependencies.
6. Installing the required packages and their dependencies based on the dependency tree.

In some cases, Composer may not be able to resolve all the dependencies automatically. This can happen when there are conflicting version constraints or dependencies that cannot be resolved. In such cases, Composer will display an error message indicating the conflict and provide suggestions on how to resolve it.

To avoid such conflicts, it is recommended to specify exact version constraints in the **composer.json** file whenever possible. This ensures that the same package versions are installed across all environments and prevents unexpected behavior due to version mismatches.

Overall, Composer's dependency resolution process makes it easy to manage complex dependency trees and ensures that all dependencies are installed correctly and consistently across different environments.

Section 4.11: Using Composer with Frameworks and CMSs

Composer is widely used in the PHP community for managing dependencies in frameworks and CMSs. Many popular PHP frameworks and CMSs, such as Laravel, Symfony, and Drupal, use Composer to manage their dependencies.

When using a framework or CMS that relies on Composer, you typically don't need to interact with Composer directly. Instead, you can use the framework or CMS's own command-line tools or web interfaces to manage your dependencies.

For example, in Laravel, you can use the composer require command to add a new package to your project, like this:

```
php artisan composer require vendor/package
```

This command is equivalent to running composer require directly, but it also updates the composer.json file and runs composer install to install the new package.

Similarly, in Drupal, you can use the composer require command to add a new module or library to your project, like this:

```
composer require drupal/module_name
```

This will add the specified module to your project and update the composer.json file.

By using Composer with frameworks and CMSs, you can take advantage of their built-in support for managing dependencies, while still enjoying the benefits of Composer's powerful dependency management capabilities.

Section 4.12: Most Common Composer Commands

Composer has several commands that are commonly used to manage dependencies in a PHP project.

Here are some of the most frequently used Composer commands:

1. **composer install**: Installs all the dependencies listed in the **composer.lock** file.
2. **composer update**: Updates all the dependencies to their latest version and creates a new **composer.lock** file.

3. **composer require**: Adds a new dependency to the project and updates the **composer.json** and **composer.lock** files.

4. **composer remove**: Removes a dependency from the project and updates the **composer.json** and **composer.lock** files.

5. **composer show**: Displays information about the installed packages.

6. **composer outdated**: Shows a list of installed packages that have newer versions available.

7. **composer self-update**: Updates the Composer itself to the latest version.

8. **composer dump-autoload**: Generates a new autoload file based on the current **composer.json** file.

9. **composer validate**: Validates the **composer.json** file to ensure it is syntactically valid.

10. **composer init**: Initializes a new **composer.json** file in the current directory.

11. **composer global require**: This command is used to install a package globally, which means it will be available to all projects on your system.

12. **composer clear-cache:** This command clears the cache and should be used when you suspect an issue with the cache.

13. **composer global remove:** This command is used to remove a package that was previously installed globally.

These commands can be executed in the terminal by navigating to the root directory of the project.

Section 4.13: Version Constraints

In order to avoid compatibility issues and ensure that the correct versions of dependencies are installed, Composer allows you to specify version constraints for each package in your composer.json file.

Version constraints in Composer are used to specify which versions of a package are acceptable for installation. These constraints are used to ensure that the required version of a package is compatible with the rest of the project's dependencies.

There are two main types of version constraints: exact constraints and range constraints.

Exact constraints allow you to specify a specific version of a package that is required for your project. This is useful when you want to ensure that a specific version of a package is used in your project, regardless of any updates that may be available. Exact constraints are specified using the syntax "package-name: version".

Example:

```
1   {
2       "require": {
3           "monolog/monolog": "1.25.3"
4       }
5   }
```

Range constraints, on the other hand, allow you to specify a range of acceptable versions for a package. This is useful when you want to allow for updates to the package, but still ensure that the updates are within a specific range of versions. Range constraints are specified using various operators.

The available operators are:

- `>` Greater than
- `<` Less than
- `>=` Greater than or equal to
- `<=` Less than or equal to
- `~` Approximately equal to
- `^` Compatible with

The `>` and `<` operators specify that the required version must be strictly greater or less than the specified version, respectively. The `>=` and `<=` operators specify that the required version must be greater than or equal to, or less than or equal to, the specified version, respectively.

The `~` operator allows for approximate matching, meaning that it allows for updates to the package, but only up to a certain point.

For example, specifying "~1.2.3" would allow for updates up to version 1.3, but not version 2.0.

The `^` operator is similar to the `~` operator, but with a slightly different behavior. It allows for updates to the package, but only up to the next major version.

For example, specifying "^1.2.3" would allow for updates up to version 2.0, but not version 3.0.

```
1   {
2       "require": {
3           "monolog/monolog": "^2.0"
4       }
5   }
```

This tells Composer to install any version of the **monolog/monolog** package that is greater than or equal to version **2.0.0**, but less than version **3.0.0**.

Section 4.14: Publishing Packages

Composer not only helps you manage dependencies, but it also makes it easy to publish your own packages. With Composer, you can create your own package, add it to Packagist, and make it available for others to use.
To create a new package, you need to create a composer.json file in the root of your project. This file should contain information about your package, such as its name, version, and dependencies.

Here is an example composer.json file for a package named "my-package":

```
1   {
2       "name": "my-vendor/my-package",
3       "description": "My Package",
4       "version": "1.0.0",
5       "license": "MIT",
6       "authors": [
7           {
8               "name": "Thusitha Avinda",
9               "email": "thusithawijethunga@gmail.com"
10          }
11      ],
12      "require": {
13          "monolog/monolog": "^2.0"
14      }
    }
```

Once you have created your package, you can add it to Packagist by following these steps:

1. Create an account on Packagist.
2. Log in to your Packagist account.
3. Click on "Submit" at the top of the page.

4. Enter the name of your package (e.g. "my-vendor/my-package").
5. Click on "Submit".
6. Wait for Packagist to index your package.

Once your package is added to Packagist, others can use it by adding it to their **composer.json** file and running composer update.

PHP Plugin, Composer.json

https://github.com/thusithawijethunga/php-plugin/blob/main/composer.json

Conclusion

In this chapter, we've explored how to manage dependencies with Composer. We've looked at how to update, install, and remove packages, how to specify specific versions, how to use private package repositories, and how to use Composer autoloading. We've also discussed how to create and publish your own packages. In the next chapter, we'll look at some best practices for managing dependencies with Composer.

5 CUSTOMIZING COMPOSER

Composer is a powerful tool that can be customized to fit your specific needs. This chapter will cover several ways to customize Composer, including using private repositories, using Composer with multiple environments, creating custom installers, creating Composer plugins, advanced Composer usage, using private packages, handling conflicts, and creating a package.

5.1 Using Private Repositories

If you are working on a project that requires packages that are not publicly available, you can use private repositories to store those packages. Composer supports several private repository options, including Satis and Packagist Private.

Private repositories can be used for a variety of reasons, such as proprietary code that cannot be shared publicly or internal packages that are not suitable for public release.

To use private repositories with Composer, you need to configure your composer.json file to include the repository URL, authentication credentials if needed, and the package name and version. The repository can be a git repository or a Composer repository.

Here is an example of a composer.json file with a private repository:

```
1  {
2      "repositories": [
3          {
4              "type": "vcs",
5              "url": "https://example.com/private-repo.git",
6              "options": {
7                  "ssh2": {
8                      "username": "your-username",
9                      "pubkey_file": "/path/to/ssh/key.pub",
10                     "privkey_file": "/path/to/ssh/key"
11                 }
12             }
13         }
14     ],
15     "require": {
16         "your-vendor/your-package": "1.0.*"
17     }
   }
```

In this example, we have defined a private repository with the URL **"https://example.com/private-repo.git"**. We have also specified the authentication credentials using SSH, which require a **username** and public/private key pair. Finally, we have required the package "your-vendor/your-package" at version "1.0.*".

Once the composer.json file has been configured, you can run the following command to install the package:

```
composer install
```

This will download the package from the private repository and install it in your project.

Private repositories can also be used to host packages that have been modified or customized for your project. In this case, you can fork the package repository, make the necessary changes, and then configure your composer.json file to use the forked repository instead of the original.

Using private repositories can help to keep your code secure and protect proprietary or sensitive information. It can also be used to manage internal packages and keep them separate from public packages.

5.1.1 Setting up a Satis Repository

Satis is a **self-hosted repository** that can be used to host private packages.

To set up a Satis repository, you will need to have a web server and PHP installed on your system. Once you have those requirements met, you can follow these steps:

1. Install Satis using Composer:

```
composer create-project composer/satis --stability=dev --keep-vcs
```

2. Create a Satis configuration file:

```
1   {
2       "name": "My Private Repository",
3       "homepage": "http://my-repo.com",
4       "repositories": [
5           {
6               "type": "vcs",
7               "url": "git@github.com:user/repo.git"
8           }
9       ],
10      "require-all": true
11  }
```

Satis, satis.json

https://github.com/thusithawijethunga/satis/blob/main/satis.json

3. Build the Satis repository:

```
php bin/satis build satis.json web/
```

4. Configure your project's **composer.json** file to use the Satis repository:

```
1   {
2       "repositories": [
3           {
4               "type": "composer",
5               "url": "http://my-repo.com"
6           }
7       ],
8       "require": {
9           "my/package": "dev-master"
10      }
11  }
```

My-Project, composer.json

https://github.com/thusithawijethunga/php-dependency-manage-
ment/blob/main/satis-repository/my-project/composer.json

5. Run composer install to install the private package.

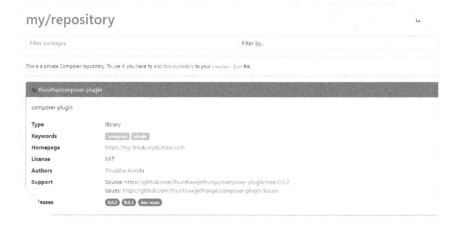

5.1.2 Using a Private Repository

If you prefer not to set up your own private repository, you can use Packagist Private to host your private packages. Packagist Private is a hosted solution that offers a private Composer repository. To use Packagist Private, you will need to sign up for an account and follow the instructions on the website to set up your private repository.

Once you have set up your private repository, you can add it to your composer.json file like this:

```
{
    "repositories": [
        {
            "type": "composer",
            "url": "https://<your-packagist-account>.packagist.com"
        }
    ],
    "require": {
        "my/package": "dev-master"
    }
}
```

5.2 Using Composer with Multiple Environments

When developing a PHP project, it's common to have multiple environments, such as production, staging, and development. Each environment may have different requirements, such as different database credentials, API keys, and other settings.

To manage dependencies across multiple environments, Composer can be used with environment-specific configuration files. This allows you to easily switch between environments while using the same set of dependencies.

5.2.1 Creating Environment-Specific Configuration Files

To create environment-specific configuration files, you can create a separate **composer.json** file for each environment that specifies the dependencies and scripts for that environment.

For example:

```
1   {
2       "require": {
3           "monolog/monolog": "^2.0"
4       },
5       "scripts": {
6           "prod": [
7               "echo 'Running production build'",
8               "composer install --no-dev"
9           ],
10          "dev": [
11              "echo 'Running development build'",
12              "composer install"
13          ],
14          "test": [
15              "echo 'Running test build'",
16              "composer install --no-dev"
17          ]
18      }
    }
```

In this example, we're using the monolog/monolog package and defining scripts for each environment (**prod**, dev, and test). (composer.prod.json, composer. dev.json, and composer.test.json)

My-Project, composer.json

https://github.com/thusithawijethunga/php-dependency-manage-ment/blob/main/satis-repository/my-project/composer.json

5.2.2 Creating Environment-Specific Configuration Files on Windows

To create environment-specific configuration files on Windows, you can create batch files for each environment that sets the **COMPOSER** environment variable to the path of the environment-specific configuration file, like this:

```
1    @echo off
2
3    REM Set the path to the Composer
4    set COMPOSER_HOME=.\prod\cache
5
6    REM Set the path to the environment-specific Composer configuration file
7    set COMPOSER=composer.prod.json
8
9    REM Run the prod script
10   composer run-script prod
```

Note that the set command is used to set the value of the **COMPOSER** environment variable to the path of the environment-specific Composer configuration file.

Also note that the **@echo off** command is used at the beginning of each file to suppress the output of each command in the batch file, making the output cleaner and easier to read.

In this example, we're setting the **COMPOSER_HOME** environment variable to the **.\prod\cache** directory, which will be used by Composer to cache packages and other data.

By using a separate cache directory for each environment, you can prevent conflicts between different versions of packages and other data that may be used in different environments.

Note that you'll need to create the **.\ prod \cache** directory before running the dev.bat file, and you'll need to create separate cache directories for each environment if you're using multiple environments.

Also note that you can customize the path to the cache directory as needed, depending on your project's directory structure and the requirements of your development environment.

My-Project, prod.bat

https://github.com/thusithawijethunga/php-dependency-management/blob/main/satis-repository/my-project/prod.bat

5.2.3 Running Environment-Specific Scripts

To run environment-specific scripts, simply execute the appropriate shell script or batch file for the environment you want to use.

For example, on Linux or macOS, you can run:

```
1   #!/bin/bash
2   export COMPOSER_HOME=./prod/cache
3   export COMPOSER=composer.prod.json
4   composer run-script prod
5
```

On Linux or macOS, you can run: **./prod.sh**, **./dev.sh** or **./test.sh**
On Windows 10, you can run: prod.bat, dev.bat or test.bat

This will run the prod, dev, or test script using the environment-specific composer.json file.

By using Composer with environment-specific configuration files, you can easily switch between environments while using the same set of dependencies. This can make it easier to manage your project's dependencies and ensure that your project works correctly in each environment.

5.3 Creating Custom Installers

Composer allows you to define custom installers for your packages. Custom installers are classes that can be used to install packages in a non-standard way, such as installing packages into a specific directory or configuring them in a particular way.

To create a custom installer, you need to create a class that extends Composer's Installer class and implement its methods. The installer should be registered in your composer.json file.

Here's an example of a custom installer class:

```php
<?php

use Composer\Installer\LibraryInstaller;

class MyInstaller extends LibraryInstaller
{
    public function install(InstalledRepositoryInterface $repo, PackageInterface $package)
    {
        parent::install($repo, $package);
        // Custom installation logic goes here
    }

    public function uninstall(InstalledRepositoryInterface $repo, PackageInterface $package)
    {
        parent::uninstall($repo, $package);
        // Custom uninstallation logic goes here
    }

    public function update(InstalledRepositoryInterface $repo, PackageInterface $initial, PackageInterface $target)
    {
        parent::update($repo, $initial, $target);
        // Custom update logic goes here
    }

    public function supports($packageType)
    {
        return $packageType === 'my-package-type';
    }
}
```

In this example, **MyInstaller** extends Composer's LibraryInstaller class, which provides a basic installation implementation. The supports() method specifies the package type that this installer should handle.

Custom Installer, MyInstaller.php

https://github.com/thusithawijethunga/template-install-er-plugin/blob/main/src/TemplateInstaller.php

Once you've created your custom installer class, you can register it in your composer.json file like this:

```
1   {
2       "name": "my/package",
3       "type": "my-package-type",
4       "require": {},
5       "extra": {
6           "installer-paths": {
7               "path/to/install": ["my/package"]
8           },
9           "class": "MyInstaller"
10      }
11  }
```

In this example, the "installer-paths" key specifies the installation path for this package, and the "class" key specifies the name of the custom installer class.

Custom Installer, Composer.json

https://github.com/thusithawijethunga/template-install-er-plugin/blob/main/composer.json

By using custom installers, you can customize the installation process of your packages and make them easier to use for your users.

This can be useful if your package requires additional steps to install, such as running database migrations or copying files to a specific location.

5.4 Creating Composer Plugins

Composer plugins are PHP classes that can be used to extend Composer's functionality. You can use plugins to add custom commands, modify the Composer installation process, or perform other custom tasks.

5.4.1 Creating a Custom Plugin

To create a custom plugin, you will need to create a PHP class that extends the **Composer\Plugin\PluginInterface** interface.

Here's an example plugin class:

```php
<?php

namespace Thusitha;

use Composer\Plugin\PluginInterface;
use Composer\Composer;
use Composer\IO\IOInterface;

class MyPlugin implements PluginInterface
{

    public function activate(Composer $composer, IOInterface $io)
    {
        $this->createLogFile($composer, $io);

        $io->write("MyPlugin activated!");
    }

    public function deactivate(Composer $composer, IOInterface $io)
    {
        $io->write("MyPlugin deactivated!");
    }

    public function uninstall(Composer $composer, IOInterface $io)
    {
        $io->write("MyPlugin uninstalled!");
    }

    private function createLogFile(Composer $composer, IOInterface $io)
    {
        $payload = [];
```

Composer Custom Installer, MyPlugin.php

https://github.com/thusithawijethunga/composer-custom-install-er/blob/main/src/MyPlugin.php

Once you have created your plugin class, you will need to register it with Composer. When Composer runs, it will load and activate your plugin.

Here's an example composer.json file for a Sample Application it using your plugin:

```
1   {
2       "name": "sample/app",
3       "require": {
4           "thusitha/my-plugin": "*",
5           "monolog/monolog": "^2.0"
6       },
7       "repositories": [
8           {
9               "type": "git",
10              "url": "https://github.com/thusithawijethunga/composer-custom-installer.git"
11          }
12      ],
13      "config": {
14          "allow-plugins": {
15              "thusitha/my-plugin": true
16          }
17      },
18      "minimum-stability": "dev",
        "prefer-stable": true
    }
```

Sample Application, composer.json

https://github.com/thusithawijethunga/php-dependency-manage-ment/blob/main/sample-app/composer.json

Here's an example Console Output after composer update in Sample Application.

```
PS D:\www\book\php-dependency-management\sample-app> composer update
Username: Thusitha Avinda
Email: thusithawijethunga@gmail.com
MyPlugin activated!
```

Here this plugin read your Current Git Username and Email address. its create sample.json file in your project directory.

```
1   {
2       "name": "Thusitha Avinda",
3       "email": "thusithawijethunga@gmail.com",
4       "app": "sample\/app",
5       "requires": {
6           "thusitha\/my-plugin": "*",
7           "monolog\/monolog": "^2.0",
8           "thusitha\/composer-plugin": "dev-main",
9           "thusitha\/php-plugin": "dev-main"
10      }
11  }
```

5.4.2 Best Practices for Creating Composer Plugins

When creating Composer plugins, it's important to follow best practices to ensure that your plugins are reliable and easy to use. Here are some best practices to keep in mind:

- Use Composer's autoloader to load your plugin classes
- Keep your plugin code simple and easy to understand
- Use Composer's events system to hook into the installation process
- Document your plugin's functionality and usage

5.4.3 Publishing a Composer Plugin

If you have created a useful Composer plugin, you may want to share it with the Composer community by publishing it to Packagist. To publish a Composer plugin, you will need to create a new package on Packagist and add the necessary information to your composer.json file.

Here's an example composer.json file for a Composer plugin:

```
1    {
2        "name": "thusitha/my-plugin",
3        "description": "My Composer plugin",
4        "type": "composer-plugin",
5        "require": {
6            "composer-plugin-api": "^2.3.0",
7            "composer/composer": "^2.5.0"
8        },
9        "autoload": {
10           "psr-4": {
11               "Thusitha\\": "src/"
12           }
13       },
14       "extra": {
15           "class": "Thusitha\\MyPlugin"
16       },
17       "minimum-stability": "dev",
18       "prefer-stable": true
     }
```

Once you have added this information to your **composer.json** file, you can publish your plugin to Packagist by running **composer update** and then **composer publish**.

SCAN ME

Composer Custom Installer, composer.json

https://github.com/thusithawijethunga/
composer-custom-installer/blob/main/composer.json

5.5 Advanced Composer Usage

In addition to the basic usage of Composer, there are several advanced techniques you can use to customize and optimize your Composer workflow.

5.5.1 Using Composer with Docker

If you work in a Docker environment, you can use Composer with Docker to ensure that your dependencies are installed consistently across all of your Docker containers. To use Composer with Docker, you will need to create a custom Docker image that includes Composer and your project dependencies.

Here's an example Dockerfile for a PHP project that uses Composer:

```
1   # syntax=docker/dockerfile:1
2
3   FROM php:7.4-fpm-alpine
4   RUN apk add --no-cache git
5   WORKDIR /var/www/html
6   COPY composer.json composer.lock ./
7   RUN composer install --prefer-dist --no-dev --no-scripts --no-progress --no-suggest
8   COPY . .
9   CMD ["php-fpm"]
10
```

In this example, we start with a base PHP image, install Git, and set the working directory to **/var/www/html**.
We then copy the **composer.json** and **composer.lock** files to the container and run composer install to install the project dependencies.
Finally, we copy the rest of the project files to the container and start the PHP-FPM process.

To build and run this Docker image, you can use the following commands:

```
docker build -t myproject . docker run -p 8080:9000 myproject
```

This will build the Docker image and start a container that exposes port 8080 and maps it to port 9000 in the container.

5.5.2 Using Composer with Continuous Integration

If you use a continuous integration (CI) system to build and test your code, you can use Composer with your CI system to ensure that your dependencies are installed correctly and consistently across all of your build environments.

Many CI systems have built-in support for Composer, such as Travis CI and CircleCI. To use Composer with your CI system, you will typically need to create a composer.json file that lists your project dependencies and a script that runs composer install.

Here's an example .travis.yml file for a PHP project that uses Composer:

```
1   language: php
2   php: - 7.4 - 8.0
3   before_script: - composer install --prefer-dist --no-dev --no-scripts --no-progress --no-suggest
4   script: - phpunit tests/
5
```

In this example,
We define two PHP versions to test against (7.4 and 8.0), and use the **before_script** section to run **composer install** to install the project dependencies. We then use the script section to run our test suite using PHPUnit.

When working on a project with multiple developers, it is important to have a continuous integration (CI) system in place to ensure that changes to the codebase do not introduce any issues. Composer can be integrated into the CI system to ensure that the correct dependencies are installed for the project.

Here are the general steps to use Composer with a CI system:

1. Configure the CI system to check out the latest codebase from the repository.
2. Install Composer on the CI system if it is not already installed.
3. Run the composer install command to install the dependencies for the project.
4. Run the project's tests to ensure that the dependencies are working correctly.
5. If the tests pass, deploy the codebase to the production environment.

Many CI systems, such as Travis CI, GitLab CI/CD, and CircleCI, have built-in support for Composer and can automatically run the composer install command as part of the build process.

These systems can also be configured to run the project's tests and deploy the codebase to the production environment.

By using Composer with a CI system, you can ensure that your project's dependencies are always up to date and that changes to the codebase do not introduce any issues.

5.6 Using Private Packages

If you have private packages that are not available on Packagist or other public repositories, you can use Composer with private repositories to manage these packages.

There are several ways to use Composer with private repositories, but one common approach is to use a tool called Satis to create a private Composer repository. **Satis** is a simple static Composer repository generator that you can use to create a repository that contains your private packages.

To use **Satis**, you will need to create a **satis.json** configuration file that lists your private packages and the URLs of the repositories that contain them. You can then use **Satis** to generate a static repository that you can host on a web server or in a private Git repository.

Once you have created your private repository, you can use Composer's config command to configure Composer to use your private repository. Here's an example composer.json file that shows how to use a private repository:

```
 1   {
 2        "repositories": [
 3            {
 4                "type": "composer",
 5                "url": "https://packagist.org"
 6            },
 7            {
 8                "type": "composer",
 9                "url": "https://my.private.repository.com"
10            }
11        ],
12        "require": {
13            "my/private-package": "dev-master"
14        }
15   }
```

In this example,
We define two repositories, one for **Packagist** and one for our private repository. We then use the require section to list our private package, **my/private-package**, and specify that we want to use the **dev-master** branch.

To configure Composer to use our private repository, we can run the following command:

```
composer config repositories.my-repo composer https://my.private.repository.com
```

This command adds our private repository to Composer's configuration, under the name **my-repo**.

To use private packages with Composer, you need to define the private package repository in the composer.json file. You can use several types of private package repositories, such as Satis, Toran Proxy, or Private Packagist.

Here is an example of how to use Private Packagist to install a private package in your project:

1. First, you need to create an account on Private Packagist and create a new repository for your private packages.
2. Once you have created a new repository, you can add your private package to it. You can either upload your package directly or connect it to a version control system like GitHub.
3. Next, you need to authenticate with Private Packagist to access your private packages. You can do this by setting your Private Packagist token in the COMPOSER_AUTH environment variable or in your global Composer configuration file.
4. Finally, you can require your private package in your project's composer.json file like you would with any other package:

```
1   {
2       "require": {
3           "private-packagist-username/private-package": "1.0.0"
4       },
5       "repositories": [
6           {
7               "type": "composer",
8               "url": "https://repo.packagist.com/private-packagist-username/"
9           }
10      ]
11  }
```

In this example,
Replace **"private-packagist-username"** with your Private Packagist username and **"private-package"** with the name of your private package. You can also specify the version of your package that you want to use.

The **"repositories"** section specifies the URL of your Private Packagist repository. You can also use other types of repositories, such as Satis or Toran Proxy, by replacing the URL with the appropriate repository URL.

Once you have added your private package to the composer.json file, you can run the **"composer install"** or **"composer update"** command to install your private package and its dependencies. Composer will automatically download your private package from your private repository and install it in your project.

5.8 Creating a Package

If you want to share your code with others or use it in multiple projects, you can create a Composer package. A Composer package is a reusable piece of code that can be installed and managed using Composer.

To create a Composer package, you will need to create a directory that contains the package code and a composer.json file that describes the package dependencies and metadata.

Here's an example composer.json file for a simple package:

```
1   {
2       "name": "my/package",
3       "description": "My package",
4       "type": "library",
5       "license": "MIT",
6       "authors": [
7           {
8               "name": "Thusitha Avinda",
9               "email": "thusithawijethunga@gmail.com"
10          }
11      ],
12      "require": {
13          "php": "^7.4"
14      },
15      "autoload": {
16          "psr-4": {
17              "My\\Package\\": "src/"
18          }
9       }
    }
```

In this example, we define the package name, description, type, license, authors, and dependencies. We also define an autoload section that tells Composer how to autoload the package code.

To create the package code, you can create a directory structure that corresponds to the autoload section of the composer.json file. In this example, we would create a src directory and a **My/Package** subdirectory.

Once you have created the package code and **composer.json** file, you can publish the package to a repository, such as Packagist, or host it in a private repository. To publish a package to Packagist, you will need to create an account on the Packagist website and follow the instructions for publishing a package.

Once your package is published, other developers can install it using Composer by adding it to their composer.json file, like this:

```
1  {
2      "require": {
3          "my/package": "^1.0"
4      }
5  }
```

This will tell Composer to download and install the **my/package** package and its dependencies.

Conclusion

Composer is a powerful tool for managing dependencies in PHP projects. It simplifies the process of installing and updating packages and makes it easy to manage dependencies across multiple projects.

In this chapter, we covered several advanced features of Composer, including using private repositories, customizing Composer with environment variables, creating custom installers and plugins, and handling conflicts. We also covered the basics of creating a Composer package and publishing it to a repository.

By mastering these advanced features of Composer, you can take your PHP development to the next level and build more complex and robust applications with ease.

6 MAVEN FOR JAVA

While Composer is a popular dependency management tool for PHP, there are similar tools available for other programming languages. In this chapter, we'll look at Maven, a dependency management tool for Java.

Section 6.1: Introduction to Maven

Maven is a build automation tool and dependency management tool for Java. It is used to manage Java projects and their dependencies, as well as to automate the build process.

Maven uses a central repository called Maven Central to store Java libraries and their dependencies. It also allows you to define your own repositories, including private repositories.

Section 6.2: Managing Dependencies with Maven

Maven uses a configuration file called pom.xml to define a project and its dependencies. In this file, you can define dependencies using the dependency element.

For example, to include the Spring Framework in your project, you can add the following code to your pom.xml file:

```
1  <dependency>
2      <groupId>org.springframework</groupId>
3      <artifactId>spring-core</artifactId>
4      <version>5.3.13</version>
5  </dependency>
```

This code defines a dependency on the spring-core artifact from the **org.springframework** group, with version **5.3.13**. When you build your project, Maven will automatically download this artifact and any of its dependencies from the configured repositories.

Section 6.3: Customizing Maven

Like Composer, Maven allows you to customize its behavior to suit your specific needs. This can be done by modifying the **pom.xml** file, as well as by using plugins and profiles.

Plugins are used to extend Maven's functionality, such as to run tests or generate documentation. Profiles allow you to define sets of configuration options that can be activated based on certain conditions, such as the environment or the build phase.

For example, to enable the **jacoco-maven-plugin** for code coverage reports, you can add the following code to your **pom.xml** file:

```
1   <build>
2       <plugins>
3           <plugin>
4               <groupId>org.jacoco</groupId>
5               <artifactId>jacoco-maven-plugin</artifactId>
6               <version>0.8.7</version>
7               <executions>
8                   <execution>
9                       <id>jacoco-report</id>
10                      <goals>
11                          <goal>report</goal>
12                      </goals>
13                  </execution>
14              </executions>
15          </plugin>
16      </plugins>
17  </build>
```

This code configures the **jacoco-maven-plugin** to run during the report phase, generating code coverage reports.

Section 6.4: Conclusion

In this book, we've explored the need for dependency management in PHP projects, and how to use Composer to manage dependencies. We've also looked at some of the ways you can customize Composer to suit your specific needs.

Finally, we've introduced Maven as a similar tool for Java projects, and looked at how to use it to manage dependencies and customize its behavior.
By mastering these tools, you can ensure that your projects have a clear and manageable dependency graph, making them easier to maintain and develop over time.

7 PIP FOR PYTHON

In addition to PHP and Java, dependency management is also an important consideration for Python projects. The most commonly used tool for managing Python dependencies is Pip.

Section 7.1: Introduction to Pip

Pip is a package installer for Python that allows you to easily install, upgrade, and uninstall packages and their dependencies. It is the de facto standard for Python package management and is included with most Python distributions.

Section 7.2: Installing Packages with Pip

To install a package using Pip, you simply need to run the pip install command followed by the name of the package.

For example, to install the requests package, you would run:

```
pip install requests
```

Pip will automatically download and install the package and any of its dependencies.

Section 7.3: Managing Packages with Pip

In addition to installing packages, Pip also provides several other commands for managing packages, including:

- **pip uninstall:** Uninstalls a package and its dependencies.
- **pip freeze:** Lists all installed packages and their versions in a format that can be used to create a requirements file.
- **pip list:** Lists all installed packages and their versions.

Section 7.4: Creating a Requirements File

A requirements file is a simple text file that lists the packages and their versions required by a project. This file can be used to easily install the required packages on another system.

To generate a requirements file, you can use the pip freeze command and redirect the output to a file.

For example, to generate a requirements file called requirements.txt, you would run:

```
pip freeze > requirements.txt
```

Section 7.5: Installing Packages from a Requirements File

To install packages from a requirements file, you simply need to run the pip install command followed by the -r option and the path to the requirements file.

For example, to install the packages listed in the requirements.txt file, you would run:

```
pip install -r requirements.txt
```

8 NPM FOR JAVASCRIPT

JavaScript is a popular language for web development, and Npm is the most commonly used tool for managing JavaScript dependencies.

Section 8.1: Introduction to Npm

Npm is a package manager for JavaScript that allows you to easily install, update, and manage dependencies for your projects. It is included with Node.js, which is a JavaScript runtime environment that allows you to run JavaScript outside of a web browser.

Section 8.2: Installing Packages with Npm

To install a package using Npm, you simply need to run the npm install command followed by the name of the package.
For example, to install the **lodash** package, you would run:

```
npm install lodash
```

Npm will automatically download and install the package and any of its dependencies.

Section 8.3: Managing Packages with Npm

In addition to installing packages, Npm also provides several other commands for managing packages, including:

- **npm uninstall:** Uninstalls a package and its dependencies.
- **npm update:** Updates all packages to their latest versions.
- **npm outdated:** Lists all packages that are out of date.
- **npm ls:** Lists all installed packages and their dependencies.

Section 8.4: Creating a Package.json File

A package.json file is a JSON file that contains information about a project, including its name, version, and dependencies. It can be used to easily install the required packages on another system.

To generate a package.json file, you can use the npm init command. This command will prompt you for information about the project, and then generate a package.json file based on your responses.

Section 8.5: Installing Packages from a Package.json File

To install packages from a package.json file, you simply need to run the npm install command. Npm will read the dependencies section of the package.json file and install all of the required packages and their dependencies.
For example, if your package.json file contained the following:

```
1  {
2      "name": "my-project",
3      "version": "1.0.0",
4      "dependencies": {
5          "lodash": "^4.17.21"
6      }
7  }
```

You could install the required packages by running:

```
npm install
```

Npm will automatically download and install the lodash package and any of its dependencies.

9 BEST PRACTICES FOR PHP DEPENDENCY MANAGEMENT

In this chapter, we will discuss best practices for managing PHP dependencies in your projects. We will provide tips for ensuring that your dependencies are up-to-date, avoiding conflicts between packages, and minimizing security vulnerabilities.

Section 9.1: Key Features of Dependency Management Tools

We will start by outlining the key features of dependency management tools, including:

- Package installation and updating
- Dependency resolution
- Customizability

Integration with build tools

Section 9.1: Keeping Dependencies Up-to-Date

One of the most important best practices for managing PHP dependencies is to keep them up-to-date. This can help ensure that your project is using the latest and most secure versions of your dependencies.

The first command you should use is **composer outdated**, which will show you a list of your dependencies that are outdated. You can run this command in your project directory to see which packages have newer versions available.

If you want to update a specific package to its latest version, you can use the **composer update** command. This command will update all packages to their latest versions by default, but you can also specify a particular package to update by providing its name as an argument.

For example,
To update the **Symfony/Console** package to its latest version, run the following command:

```
composer update symfony/console
```

Alternatively, you can update all packages to their latest versions using the **composer update** command without any arguments.

It's also possible to update packages to a specific version.

For example,
If you want to update the **Symfony/Console** package to version **4.4**, you can run the following command:

```
composer update symfony/console:4.4
```

After running any update command, it's essential to test your project thoroughly to ensure that everything still works as expected. You should also commit your changes to your version control system to keep track of the updates you have made.

Another best practice for keeping dependencies up-to-date is to regularly check for updates and security patches for your dependencies. You can do this by subscribing to mailing lists or following the social media accounts of the package maintainers.

Finally, you can automate the process of keeping your dependencies up-to-date by running composer update regularly or using a continuous integration tool like Travis CI to automatically run tests and update dependencies when new versions become available.

Section 9.2: Comparison of Dependency Management Tools

We will then compare the four tools covered in this book based on these key features. We will examine the differences in syntax, functionality, and performance.

Section 9.2: Avoiding Dependency Conflicts

Another important best practice for managing PHP dependencies is to avoid conflicts between packages. Dependency conflicts can occur when two or more packages require different versions of the same package.

To avoid conflicts, you can use Composer's built-in update command with the --with-dependencies option. This will update all packages in your project and their dependencies, ensuring that all packages are compatible with each other:

```
composer update --with-dependencies
```

Another best practice for avoiding conflicts is to carefully review the composer.lock file. This file contains a list of all the packages and their exact versions that were installed in your project. You can review this file to ensure that all packages are compatible with each other.

Section 9.3: Choosing the Right Tool for the Job

Finally, we will discuss when you might want to choose one tool over the other. We will provide use case examples for each tool and discuss the tradeoffs of using each one.

Section 9.3: Minimizing Security Vulnerabilities

Minimizing security vulnerabilities in your PHP dependencies is another important best practice. This can help protect your project from security threats such as hacking and malware.

To minimize security vulnerabilities, you should regularly check for security patches and updates for your dependencies. You can do this by subscribing to mailing lists or following the social media accounts of the package maintainers.

Another best practice for minimizing security vulnerabilities is to use

Composer's built-in validate command. This command will check the composer.json file for any security vulnerabilities in the packages you have installed:

```
composer validate
```

You can also use Composer's built-in outdated command to check for outdated packages:

```
composer outdated
```

Section 9.4: Conclusion

In this chapter, we have discussed best practices for managing PHP dependencies in your projects. By keeping your dependencies up-to-date, avoiding conflicts between packages, and minimizing security vulnerabilities, you can ensure that your project is using the latest and most secure packages available.

10 MANAGING DEPENDENCIES IN LARGE-SCALE PROJECTS

In this chapter, we will discuss the unique challenges of managing dependencies in large-scale PHP projects. We will provide tips for organizing and structuring your project to minimize conflicts and ensure scalability.

Section 10.1: Keeping Dependencies Up-to-Date

We will discuss the importance of keeping your dependencies up-to-date and provide tips for automating the process of updating packages.

Section 10.1: Dependency Management Strategies

When managing dependencies in a large-scale PHP project, it's important to have a well-defined dependency management strategy.

This includes:

1. **Version control:** Using a version control system such as Git to manage your codebase and dependencies.
2. **Repository management:** Using a repository management system such as Artifactory or Nexus to store and manage your dependencies.
3. **Code review:** Conducting code reviews to ensure that all changes to the codebase and dependencies are reviewed and approved by team members.
4. **Continuous integration:** Implementing a continuous integration (CI) system such as Jenkins or Travis CI to automatically build and

test your project after each code change.

5. **Automated testing:** Implementing automated testing to ensure that your project works as expected after each code change.

By implementing these strategies, you can ensure that your project is scalable and maintainable.

Section 10.2: Avoiding Dependency Conflicts

We will discuss the potential for conflicts between packages and provide tips for managing dependencies to avoid conflicts.

Section 10.2: Organizing Dependencies

In a large-scale PHP project, it's important to organize your dependencies in a way that minimizes conflicts and ensures scalability.

This can be done by:

1. **Using namespaces:** Using namespaces to organize your project's classes and dependencies.
2. **Using dependency injection:** Using dependency injection to manage dependencies between classes.
3. **Using Composer's autoloader:** Using Composer's autoloader to automatically load classes and dependencies.
4. **Using PSR standards:** Following PSR standards for coding and dependency management.

By organizing your dependencies in a logical and structured way, you can minimize conflicts and ensure scalability.

Section 10.3: Minimizing Security Vulnerabilities

We will discuss the importance of minimizing security vulnerabilities in your dependencies and provide tips for staying on top of security patches and updates.

Section 10.3: Maintaining Compatibility

Maintaining compatibility between dependencies is crucial in a large-scale PHP project. This can be challenging when working with many different packages and versions.

To maintain compatibility, you should:

1. **Regularly update dependencies:** Keeping your dependencies up-to-date can ensure that they are compatible with each other.
2. **Use stable releases:** Using stable releases of packages can help ensure that they are compatible with your project.
3. **Test dependencies together:** Testing dependencies together can help ensure that they are compatible with each other.
4. **Use version constraints:** Using version constraints in your composer.json file can help ensure that your dependencies are compatible with each other.
5.

By maintaining compatibility between dependencies, you can ensure that your project is scalable and maintainable.

Section 10.4: Conclusion

In this chapter, we have discussed the unique challenges of managing dependencies in large-scale PHP projects. By implementing a well-defined dependency management strategy, organizing dependencies in a logical way, and maintaining compatibility between dependencies, you can ensure that your project is scalable and maintainable.

11 CASE STUDY: DEPENDENCY MANAGEMENT IN WORDPRESS

In this chapter, we will take a closer look at how dependency management is handled in WordPress, one of the most popular content management systems (CMS) built with PHP.

Section 11.1: Background

WordPress is a free and open-source CMS that powers over 40% of all websites on the internet. It was first released in 2003 and has since grown to become a highly customizable platform with a vast array of plugins and themes available for users to extend its functionality.

WordPress is built with PHP and uses a number of third-party libraries and packages to provide its core functionality.

Section 11.2: Dependency Management in WordPress

WordPress uses a combination of manual and automated dependency management to ensure that its codebase is maintainable and scalable.

WordPress's dependency management system includes:

1. **A custom-built package manager:** WordPress includes its own package manager, which allows developers to easily install and manage third-party packages.
2. **The use of Composer:** WordPress uses Composer to manage dependencies for its REST API and other components.

3. **A strict backwards compatibility policy:** WordPress has a strict policy of maintaining backwards compatibility, which ensures that new versions of the CMS do not break existing plugins and themes.
4. **Manual review of plugins and themes:** WordPress's review team manually reviews all plugins and themes submitted to the WordPress repository, ensuring that they are secure and adhere to best practices.

By using these strategies, WordPress is able to ensure that its codebase is maintainable and scalable, while also providing a high degree of flexibility to developers.

Section 11.3: Challenges and Opportunities

While WordPress's dependency management system is generally effective, there are some challenges and opportunities for improvement.

One of the main challenges is the sheer number of plugins and themes available for WordPress. This can make it difficult to ensure that all third-party code is secure and adheres to best practices.

There is also an opportunity to further streamline WordPress's dependency management system by relying more heavily on Composer and other industry-standard tools.

Section 11.4: Conclusion

WordPress's dependency management system provides a good example of how a large-scale PHP project can effectively manage dependencies. By using a combination of manual and automated techniques, WordPress is able to ensure that its codebase is maintainable and scalable, while also providing a high degree of flexibility to developers. However, there are still challenges and opportunities for improvement, particularly with regards to managing the large number of third-party plugins and themes available for the platform.

12 CASE STUDY: DEPENDENCY MANAGEMENT IN LARAVEL

In this chapter, we will examine how Laravel, a popular PHP web application framework, approaches dependency management.

Section 12.1: Background

Laravel is a free and open-source web application framework that was first released in 2011. It is built with PHP and provides a wide range of features for developing modern web applications, including routing, middleware, authentication, and more.

Laravel relies heavily on third-party packages to provide its functionality, and uses a variety of tools and techniques to manage these dependencies.

Section 12.2: Dependency Management in Laravel

Laravel's dependency management system includes:

1. **Composer:** Laravel uses Composer as its primary dependency manager, and all of its dependencies are managed through Composer packages.
2. **Service Providers:** Laravel uses Service Providers to register and bootstrap third-party packages, providing a clean and modular architecture.
3. **Facades:** Laravel uses Facades to provide a simple and expressive way of accessing functionality provided by third-party packages.

4. **Versioning:** Laravel uses Semantic Versioning to manage the versioning of its packages and ensure compatibility between different versions.

By using these strategies, Laravel is able to provide a flexible and extensible framework while also maintaining a high level of maintainability and scalability.

Section 12.3: Challenges and Opportunities

While Laravel's dependency management system is generally effective, there are still some challenges and opportunities for improvement.

One of the main challenges is the potential for version conflicts between different third-party packages. This can be mitigated through careful version management and testing, but can still present challenges for developers.

There is also an opportunity to further improve Laravel's dependency management system by exploring new tools and techniques, such as containerization and automated testing.

Section 12.4: Conclusion

Laravel's dependency management system provides a good example of how a modern PHP framework can effectively manage dependencies. By relying on industry-standard tools like Composer and adopting modular design patterns like Service Providers and Facades, Laravel is able to provide a flexible and extensible framework while also maintaining a high level of maintainability and scalability. However, there are still challenges and opportunities for improvement, particularly with regards to versioning and testing.

13 DEPENDENCY RESOLUTION AND CONFLICT RESOLUTION

In this chapter, we will discuss the concepts of dependency resolution and conflict resolution in the context of PHP dependency management.

Section 13.1: Dependency Resolution

Dependency resolution is the process of identifying and resolving the dependencies required by a software package. In PHP, this is typically done through the use of a dependency manager like Composer.

When a package is installed via Composer, it will analyze the package's dependencies and recursively install any additional packages required to satisfy those dependencies. This process is known as dependency resolution.

Dependency resolution can be a complex process, particularly in large projects with many interdependent packages. However, by relying on a robust dependency manager like Composer, developers can ensure that all required dependencies are installed and configured correctly.

Section 13.2: Conflict Resolution

Conflict resolution is the process of identifying and resolving conflicts between different packages and their dependencies. Conflicts can arise when two packages have conflicting requirements for a shared dependency, or when a package requires a specific version of a dependency that is not compatible with other packages in the project.

In PHP, conflict resolution is typically handled by Composer, which uses a variety of strategies to identify and resolve conflicts between packages. These strategies may include downgrading or upgrading dependencies, or selecting a different version of a package that is compatible with all other dependencies in the project.

Conflict resolution can be a time-consuming process, particularly in large projects with many dependencies. However, by relying on a robust dependency manager like Composer and adopting best practices for dependency management, developers can minimize the risk of conflicts and ensure that their projects are stable and maintainable.

Section 13.3: Best Practices for Dependency and Conflict Resolution

To effectively manage dependencies and avoid conflicts, it is important to follow best practices for dependency management. These include:

1. Use a robust dependency manager like Composer to handle package installation and management.
2. Regularly update packages to ensure that dependencies are up-to-date and compatible with each other.
3. Carefully manage package versions to avoid conflicts and ensure compatibility between different packages.
4. Adopt modular design patterns and use service providers and facades to minimize interdependencies between packages.

By following these best practices, developers can ensure that their projects are stable, maintainable, and free from conflicts.

Section 13.4: Conclusion

Dependency resolution and conflict resolution are essential components of effective PHP dependency management. By relying on robust dependency managers like Composer and adopting best practices for dependency management, developers can minimize the risk of conflicts and ensure that their projects are stable and maintainable.

14 MANAGING PRIVATE PACKAGES AND REPOSITORIES

In this chapter, we will discuss the management of private packages and repositories in the context of PHP dependency management.

Section 14.1: Private Packages

A private package is a package that is not publicly available on a package registry like Packagist. Private packages are often used for proprietary code or code that is not intended for public consumption.

Managing private packages can be a challenge, particularly in large projects with many contributors. However, there are several strategies that can be used to simplify the process, including:

1. **Creating a private repository:** One option is to create a private repository that is accessible only to authorized users. This repository can be hosted on a private server or a cloud-based service like GitHub.
2. **Using version control:** Another strategy is to use version control software like Git to manage private packages. This can simplify the process of tracking changes and collaborating with other contributors.
3. **Using a private package manager:** There are also several private package managers available, such as Private Packagist, that allow organizations to manage their own private packages and repositories.

Section 14.2: Private Repositories

A private repository is a repository that is not publicly available on a code-sharing platform like GitHub or Bitbucket. Private repositories are often used for proprietary code or code that is not intended for public consumption.

Managing private repositories can be a challenge, particularly in large projects with many contributors. However, there are several strategies that can be used to simplify the process, including:

1. **Using a private code-sharing platform:** One option is to use a private code-sharing platform like GitHub Enterprise or Bitbucket Server. These platforms allow organizations to host their own private repositories and manage access for authorized users.
2. **Using access controls:** Another strategy is to use access controls to restrict access to private repositories. This can be done by setting permissions for individual users or groups of users.
3. **Using a private package manager:** As mentioned in section 14.1, private package managers like Private Packagist can also be used to manage private repositories.

Section 14.3: Best Practices for Managing Private Packages and Repositories

To effectively manage private packages and repositories, it is important to follow best practices for package management. These include:

1. Using a private repository or code-sharing platform to host private packages and repositories.
2. Using version control software like Git to manage changes and collaborate with other contributors.
3. Implementing access controls to restrict access to private packages and repositories.
4. Regularly updating packages to ensure that dependencies are up-to-date and compatible with each other.
5. Adhering to best practices for package versioning and dependency management.

By following these best practices, developers can ensure that their private

93

packages and repositories are secure, stable, and maintainable.

Section 14.4: Conclusion

Managing private packages and repositories can be a challenge, particularly in large projects with many contributors. However, by using a private repository or code-sharing platform, implementing access controls, and following best practices for package versioning and dependency management, developers can ensure that their private packages and repositories are secure, stable, and maintainable.

15 CONTINUOUS INTEGRATION AND DEPLOYMENT

In modern software development, continuous integration (CI) and continuous deployment (CD) are crucial for ensuring the quality and reliability of software. The use of automated tools for building, testing, and deploying code can greatly improve the efficiency of the development process and minimize errors caused by manual processes. In this chapter, we will discuss how to integrate PHP dependency management into a CI/CD pipeline, including best practices and tools that can be used.

Section 15.1: Continuous Integration

Continuous integration is the practice of frequently merging code changes into a shared repository and running automated tests to detect any errors or conflicts. The goal of CI is to catch problems early in the development process, before they cause larger issues downstream.

In a PHP project, the first step in setting up a CI pipeline is to define the required dependencies and install them using Composer. This ensures that the required packages are available for building and testing the code. Once the dependencies are installed, the next step is to run automated tests.

There are several testing frameworks available for PHP, including **PHPUnit, Behat**, and **Codeception**. These frameworks provide a variety of testing capabilities, including unit testing, functional testing, and acceptance testing. To incorporate testing into a CI pipeline, it is important to define a set of tests that can be run automatically on each code change.

In addition to running tests, a CI pipeline can also include steps for code linting and code style checking. These steps can help ensure that code adheres to established coding standards and best practices.

Section 15.2: Continuous Deployment

Continuous deployment is the practice of automatically deploying code changes to a production environment. In order to achieve continuous deployment, it is important to have a well-defined release process that includes versioning and tagging of releases, as well as deployment automation.

In a PHP project, the use of Composer can greatly simplify the process of managing dependencies in a production environment. By including a composer.lock file in the code repository, it is possible to ensure that the same versions of packages are installed in both development and production environments. This helps minimize the risk of unexpected behavior due to version differences.

There are several deployment tools available for PHP projects, including Jenkins, Travis CI, and CircleCI. These tools can be used to automate the deployment process, including tasks such as building the code, running tests, and deploying to production.

Section 15.3: Best Practices

When incorporating PHP dependency management into a CI/CD pipeline, there are several best practices that should be followed:

- Define a clear process for managing dependencies and updating packages. This should include guidelines for versioning, package selection, and dependency resolution.
- Use automated tools for building, testing, and deployment. This helps ensure that code changes are tested thoroughly and deployed consistently.
- Use a package manager such as Composer to manage dependencies. This helps simplify the process of installing and updating packages.

- Use a locking mechanism such as a composer.lock file to ensure that the same versions of packages are installed in both development and production environments.
- Define a set of tests that can be run automatically on each code change. This helps ensure that changes do not introduce unexpected behavior.
- Use a code style checker and linter to ensure that code adheres to established standards and best practices.

Section 15.4: Conclusion

In this chapter, we discussed the importance of incorporating PHP dependency management into a CI/CD pipeline. By using automated tools and best practices for managing dependencies, it is possible to improve the efficiency and reliability of software development. Additionally, the use of a package manager such as Composer can greatly simplify the process of managing dependencies in both development and production environments.

Reference and Resources:

- ✓ Composer:
  - o https://getcomposer.org/
- ✓ Laravel Composer:
  - o https://laravel.com/docs/10.x/installation#your-first-laravel-project

Sample Source code:

- ✓ GitHub:
  - o https://github.com/thusithawijethunga/php-dependency-management.git

Php Dependency Management.git

https://github.com/thusithawijethunga/php-dependency-management.git

Thanks,

You're welcome! The PHP community and its contributors have worked hard to create a robust and powerful language that is widely used for web development. Their efforts have helped make PHP a key player in the development of dynamic websites and web applications. I'm sure that the future of PHP will continue to be bright, with new features, libraries, and tools being developed to enhance its capabilities.

ABOUT W G T AVINDA

W G T Avinda is a Full Stack Developer and web developer with over 11 years of experience working with PHP. He has extensive experience in designing websites and developing mobile apps using IONIC Angular-based frameworks.

W G T Avinda's technical skills include:

- Progressive Web Apps Development.
- Ionic Mobile App Development.
- Digitalocean Cloud System.
- Arduino, Internet of Things (IoT) with Wi-Fi Module.
- Laravel Framework PHP Development.
- Node Package Management and Composer Package Management.
- Versioning, Branching, and Tag Management for SCM.
- Continuous Integration with Git and Jenkins.
- JavaScript, Animation, Sliders, and Validation.
- Designing and Developing Mobile REST APIs.

W G T Avinda is passionate about using technology to solve problems and has a track record of delivering high-quality software solutions. He has worked on a wide range of projects, from small startups to large enterprises, and is adept at adapting to new technologies and requirements.

When he's not coding, W G T Avinda enjoys hiking and spending time with his family. You can learn more about him and his work by visiting his website at wgtavinda.me.

Thank you for choosing "Getting Started with PHP 8", and we hope you find the book helpful in your PHP development journey.

www.ingramcontent.com/pod-product-compliance
Lightning Source LLC
LaVergne TN
LVHW051710050326
832903LV00032B/4108